REGION Volume 5, Number 2, 2018

# Urban Freight, land use planning and public administration strategies

Special Issue edited by **Edoardo Marcucci**, **Valerio Gatta**, and **Laetitia Dablanc**

## Table of Contents

### Editorials



### Articles

This special issue on "Urban Freight, land use planning and public administration strategies" is edited by Edoardo Marcucci (University Roma 3, Rome, Italy), Valerio Gatta (University of Roma 3, Rome, Italy), and Laetitia Dablanc (University of Paris-East, Paris, France). With the exception of the editorial, all contributions to this special issue have already been published in earlier issues of REGION, for the sake of immediate exposure of the content.

- *European urban freight transport policies and research funding: are priorities and Horizon 2020 calls aligned?* by Giacomo Lozzi, Valerio Gatta, Edoardo Marcucci was originally published in vol. 5, no. 1, 53–71.

- *Logistics sprawl in monocentric and polycentric metropolitan areas: the cases of Paris, France, and the Randstad, the Netherlands* by Adeline Heitz, Laetitia Dablanc, Lorant A. Tavasszy was originally published in vol. 4, no. 1, 93–107.

- *Potentials and limitations for the use of accessibility measures for national transport policy goals in freight transport and logistics: evidence from Västra Götaland County, Sweden* by Anders Larsson, Jerry Olsson was originally published in vol. 4, no. 1, 71–92.

- *Analysis of Freight Trip Generation Model for Food and Beverage in Belo Horizonte (Brazil)* by Leise Kelli de Oliveira, Rodrigo Affonso de Albuquerque Nóbrega, Daniel Gonçalves Ebias, Bruno Gomes e Souza Corrêa was originally published in vol. 4, no. 1, 17–30.

**REGION, The journal of ERSA / Powered by WU**
ISSN: 2409-5370, ISBN: 978-3-9504846-1-8

ERSA: http://www.ersa.org
WU: http://www.wu.ac.at

# Editorials

Volume 5, Number 2, 2018, E1–E3
DOI: 10.18335/region.v5i2.244

journal homepage: region.ersa.org

# Editorial:
# Urban Freight, land use planning and public administration strategies

Edoardo Marcucci[1], Valerio Gatta[1], Laetitia Dablanc[2]

[1] University Roma 3, Rome, Italy
[2] University of Paris-East, Paris, France

Received: 20 March 2018/Accepted: 26 March 2018

**Abstract.** This editorial introduces the special issue on "Urban Freight, land use planning and public administration strategies". In the first part, it describes the rationale for the special issue and motivates the choice of focusing on land use planning and public administration strategies in the urban freight transportation context. In the second part, the editorial illustrates the specific contributions provided by the research papers included in the special issue showing the diversity of policy questions urban freight entails. It demonstrates how big is the gap between what is needed to provide a well-developed framework for fostering sustainable urban freight and what is actually known.

## 1 Why this special issue?

Well-being and economic growth are strictly correlated. Cities are the engines of an innovation-based economy where research and new ideas are the core input of production. Urbanisation is becoming synonymous with economic growth. People flock into cities, both in the developed and developing world, since that is where wealth is, where high quality services are available and life standards are comparatively higher than other places. However, one has to acknowledge that growth also produces undesired negative effects. In fact, cities are net importers. They need to acquire consumption/intermediate goods, export production and get rid of waste. In other words, the existence of a city relies on a transportation system providing the necessary services for its functioning. The typical urban transportation system heavily depends on passenger and freight movements by road. While this dependency is, in some cases, less relevant for passenger transport, most of the freight moved in, out, within and through a city relies on motorized road transportation. Trucks and vans are responsible for congestion, polluting emissions, accidents, noise, visual intrusion and stench. All these negative effects are concentrated where many citizens live and, consequently, produce relevant economic (e.g. time lost), environmental (e.g. air quality), and social (e.g. segregation) impacts. Cities, in order to be attractive, sustainable and thriving, need an efficient freight transportation system. Fast changing consumption patterns with the rise of e-commerce and home deliveries also points to another dimension of cities: their need to adapt quickly to economic trends.

Land use planning and public administration strategies potentially have relevant impacts on urban freight transportation, which one has always to remember, is a derived demand. Developing dense neighbourhoods characterised by high attractiveness, accessibility and sustainability can provide viable solutions to foster sustainable passenger and freight mobility. City shape and functional organisation has strong implications with respect to how much freight is demanded and how its distribution is organised and performed.

Local authorities face daunting challenges in developing tailored intervention policies aimed at stimulating a smart urban development. Acknowledging these challenges, the European Commission has suggested the adoption of the Sustainable Urban Mobility Planning approach, which is one of the most important topics proposed within the Commission's Urban Mobility Package. The Sustainable Urban Mobility Plan considers a city as a single functional urban area and auspices its development in a cooperative fashion across different policy areas, sectors and levels of government assuming an active role for citizens and other stakeholders. The Commission supports the development of Sustainable Urban Mobility Plans through funding instruments and information provision while acknowledging the relevance of local policymaking and in full respect of the subsidiarity principle. It supports the adoption of best practices and finances innovative applied research via dedicated research programs among which Horizon 2020 plays a major role.

## 2  The papers in this special issue

The papers in this special issue address, from alternative points of view and using different methodological approaches, some of the relevant and critical issues pertaining to land use planning and administration strategies in modern cities with respect to the urban freight sector.

In fact, the first paper of this issue by Lozzi, Gatta and Marcucci titled "European urban freight transport policies and research funding: are priorities and H2020 calls aligned?" investigates the correlation between the policy priorities about urban freight stated at a European level and the provision of research funding. Transport is a shared responsibility between the European Union and the Member States, where the subsidiarity principle applies. Accordingly, the European Commission provides local authorities with support in different areas, including research and innovation funding. This paper aims to assess the linkage and consistency between European policy priorities for urban freight transport and the corresponding calls of the Horizon 2020 Research Programme, created by the European Commission to foster research and innovation. The paper identifies and extrapolates in a comparable format 10 urban freight priority solutions and estimates their degree of correspondence with the Horizon 2020 Work Programmes, using the amount of research funds allocated to each of them as a proxy. Findings show that, generally, the European Commission addresses urban freight transport through a systematic and coherent approach. Moreover, all the identified solutions are covered by at least one Horizon 2020 call, although the extent of the coverage is heterogeneous.

Heitz, Dablanc and Tavasszy with a paper titled "Logistics sprawl in monocentric and polycentric metropolitan areas: the cases of Paris, France, and the Randstad, the Netherlands" delve into the logistic sprawl issue in a comparative fashion. In fact, urban sprawl has been extensively studied with a focus on residential settlements while little attention, so far, has been given to the freight-related part of the issue. The paper explicitly addresses logistic sprawl, which manifests itself via the growth and suburban relocation of warehousing activities. More specifically, it investigates the difference in logistic sprawl between monocentric and polycentric city systems. Literature suggests that logistics activities will gradually migrate to suburbs since land prices rise in central areas. Logistic geography research has mostly focused on monocentric systems and the research question this paper asks is to what extent this also applies to polycentric ones. The paper compares the Paris region in France, representative of a monocentric urban development, with the Dutch Randstad area as a polycentric case. Regional statistics on warehouse settlements in both regions provide a description of changes in concentration since the mid-2000s. The comparison underlines heterogeneous variations. In fact, in contrast to Paris, logistics activities within the Randstad have become more intense in dense areas. The paper suggests that reasons explaining the difference include urban structure, spatial planning policies, and the existence of large freight hubs such as the port of Rotterdam.

The paper by Larsson and Olsson, titled "Potentials and limitations for the use of accessibility measures for national transport policy goals in freight transport and logistics: Evidence from Vastra Gotaland County" reports on a pilot study investigating the potential to develop accessibility measures to support and follow up policy objectives in the Swedish Context. In fact, while Swedish national transport policy considers freight transport as a facilitator of economic development at all geographical levels, it is also suggested by the Authors that methods and data for business location and transportation are inadequate for following up transport policy objectives. The paper discusses and problematizes the concept of accessibility and its application in concrete measures using several practical examples from Vastra Gotaland County. The paper identifies several potentials and limitations linked to the use of accessibility measures to address freight transport issues. The usefulness of these measures mainly rests on the possible integration of transport and land use, thus asking questions that are more complex and developing better measures while supporting the integration between planning specializations. Limitations largely relate to data availability, quality and the extent to which one can purposely communicate maps/measures to non-experts. Conclusions highlight the centrality of policy and governance context in understanding and using the concept of accessibility and its related measures.

Finally, the paper by de Oliveira, de Albuquerque, Nobrega, Ebias, Gomes and Correa titled "Analysis of Freight Trip Generation Model for Food and Beverage in Belo Horizonte (Brazil)" investigates, in the case of Brazil, the negative consequences of unplanned urban sprawl as well as the lack of adequate transport infrastructure. The paper reports the results of a freight-trip generation model developed for pubs and restaurants in Belo Horizonte (Brazil). Data on goods, frequency, operation time, place of performance of the loading/unloading of goods, establishment size and the number of employees were obtained via a survey based on a structured questionnaire. The estimation of a linear regression allows for investigating the relationship between the number of trips and: i) establishment, ii) number of employees, and iii) operation day of the establishment. The results provide sample classification bands that were analysed together with other geographic data such as demographic data, road network density and socioeconomic data. Findings underline the importance that a mathematic-geographic model for trip generation might have in supporting transportation planning and operation for urban goods distribution. The research also highlights the need for an urban freight mobility plan and dedicated public policies to promote sustainable alternatives for urban goods distribution. Using geospatial analysis, the study produces useful statistics and maps to support decision makers and transportation managers in their discussion about policymaking priorities aimed at fostering sustainable freight logistic operations in Belo Horizonte.

The research papers reported in this special issue show the diversity of policy questions urban freight entails. They show how relevant and important the investigation of land use policies and local administration strategies are, how difficult it is to deal with them and, finally, how big the gap between what is needed to provide a well-developed framework for fostering sustainable urban freight and what is actually known. This special issue represents an attempt to catalyze good research efforts and knowledge creation around critical but under-researched issues in the urban freight sector. Hopefully this attempt will stimulate scholars to engage in other similar projects aimed at pursuing the research goals that the Guest Editors of this special issue had in mind when accepting the challenge of joining forces for this endeavour.

# Articles

REGION

The Journal of ERSA
Powered by WU

Volume 5, Number 1, 2018, 53–71
DOI: 10.18335/region.v5i1.168

journal homepage: region.ersa.org

# European urban freight transport policies and research funding: are priorities and Horizon 2020 calls aligned?

Giacomo Lozzi[1], Valerio Gatta[1], Edoardo Marcucci[2]

[1] University Roma 3, Rome, Italy
[2] Molde University, Norway

Received: 17 October 2016/Accepted: 26 February 2018

**Abstract.** The European Commission has recently developed a growing awareness with respect to the challenges urban freight transport (UFT) poses to cities and, consequently, has started defining specific policies and promoting dedicated tools to address them. Transport is a shared responsibility between the European Union and the Member States, where the subsidiarity principle applies. Accordingly, the former provides European local authorities with support in different areas, including research and innovation funding. This paper aims to assess the linkage and consistency between European policy priorities for UFT and the corresponding calls of the Horizon 2020 (H2020) Research Programme, created to foster research and innovation. The paper identifies and extrapolates in a comparable format ten UFT priority solutions and estimates their degree of correspondence with the H2020 Work Programmes using the amount of research funds allocated to each of them as a proxy. Findings show that, generally, the European Commission addresses UFT through a systematic and coherent approach. Moreover, all the identified solutions are covered by at least one H2020 call, although the extent of the coverage is heterogeneous. Four of the UFT solutions present an overall consistency when it comes to comparing the extent of the scope of the solution and the number of policy documents addressing it, on the one hand, and the number of calls considering it and the budget (potentially) available, on the other.

**Key words:** Horizon 2020, urban mobility, urban freight transport, European Union, transport policy

## 1 Urban freight transport challenges and opportunities for research

European cities host 72% of the European Union population (80% in 2020) and generate over 80% of its GDP. About 25% of CO2 emissions produced in urban areas are attributable to the transport sector, as well as 30-50% of other transport-related pollutants, such as particulate matters and Nitrogen Oxide (ALICE/ERTRAC 2014). Congestion causes inefficiencies producing losses of around 80 billion €per year (European Commission 2011). The 2011 White Paper on Transport identifies the need to take additional steps to ensure that cities contribute to reducing Europe's dependence on imported oil and cutting carbon emissions in transport by 60% by 2050 and achieving essentially CO2-free city logistics in major urban centres by 2030 (European Commission 2011).

During the last two decades, the European Commission has developed a growing awareness with respect to the challenges of the urban transport sector, and, consequently, has started defining specific policies and developing dedicated tools to tackle them. Transport is a shared responsibility between the European Union and Member States (MSs) where the subsidiarity principle[1] applies. Urban mobility is essentially a local responsibility. However, in the light of the challenges mentioned above, there is an increasing demand for strengthening cooperation. In fact, urban mobility policies are too heterogeneous, both between and within MSs. For this reason, the European Union provides local authorities with support in the following areas: i) setting a common policy framework; ii) funding for implementation; iii) funding for research and innovation; iv) facilitating the exchange of experience and best practice; v) raising awareness.

Concentration of economic activities and population in European cities are both high and rising. The two phenomena produce new challenges for goods distribution. Public authorities have recently developed a growing, yet still insufficient, awareness of the crucial role urban freight transport (UFT)[2] policies play within the overall urban mobility system. European MSs need to further integrate UFT in the general city mobility management system. The European Commission is setting up coordinated UFT initiatives and actions. One of these supporting actions is to promote research and innovation to deliver innovative and effective solutions to tackle urban mobility challenges. This is realised through Horizon 2020 (H2020), the European research and innovation programme for the period 2014-2020.

This paper aims to identify the most important UFT policy solutions proposed in the relevant European policy documents, and to evaluate how policy priorities result in funding. In more detail, the paper describes UFT challenges for policy-makers and how policy priorities are defined and assesses whether H2020 funds are consistently allocated to the identified UFT policy solutions according to the weight attributed to UFT in the policy documents.

The paper is structured as follows: section 2 illustrates the methodological steps and the logic behind the analyses performed. Section 3 discusses the main topics and the corresponding solutions reported in the policy documents with respect to UFT. Section 4 shows the results of the consistency evaluation between policy priorities and research funding. Section 5 concludes highlighting future research endeavours.

## 2   Methodology

The methodology adopted consists of three main steps: (1) selecting policy documents; (2) identifying the most relevant UFT policy solutions; (3) assessing consistency between policy priorities and H2020 research funding.

Three criteria have been used for selecting policy documents. The first criterion refers to the type of documents. A premise on legal aspects is necessary to motivate the choice made. At European level, there are various forms of action: recommendations, directives, communications and acts concerning the organization and functioning of the institutions. Their qualification, structure and legal effects result from various provisions of the treaties or the rules adopted in their application. Also of note is the importance of White Papers[3], Green Papers[4] and Action programmes, through which agreements

---

[1]Its legal basis is Article 5(3) of the Treaty on European Union (TEU): "Under the principle of subsidiarity, in areas which do not fall within its exclusive competence, the Union shall act only if and in so far as the objectives of the proposed action cannot be sufficiently achieved by the Member States, either at central level or at regional and local level, but can rather, by reason of the scale or effects of the proposed action, be better achieved at Union level".

[2]The European Commission defines UFT as "the movement of freight vehicles whose primary purpose is to carry goods into, out of and within urban areas" (MDS 2012). But the it also provides a very similar definition of 'urban logistics': "[...] the movement of goods, equipment and waste into, out, from, within or through an urban area" (European Commission 2013a). For this reason, the choice here is to consider the two expressions as synonyms and to use only "UFT", systematically replacing "urban logistics" with "UFT" every time the research incurred in the former expression.

[3]White Papers communicate a decided Commission policy or approach on a particular issue. They are chiefly intended as statements of Commission policy, rather than a consultation or starting point for debate.

[4]Green Papers are usually used to launch a consultation process. They present Commission policy orientations for debate to interested parties who may wish to comment. The Commission will generally prepare a subsequent proposal.

on long-term objectives among MSs are made. The European Commission prepares and publishes guidance documents relating to the areas over which it has (full or residual) jurisdiction. In the case of urban mobility, the binding power resides in the hands of the MSs, but, in some cases and for certain types of actions, the European Union can intervene through the subsidiarity principle. Since the aim of the paper is to focus on the relationship between UFT policies and the research programmes financed by H2020, the types of acts considered are non-binding guidelines, which can take different forms (e.g. White Papers, Green Papers, Communications[5]), while binding legislative provisions are out of the scope.

The second criterion relates to the field considered. European policies, when addressing any area where concrete intervention is required, very often imply a certain overlapping with other fields. For example, the White Paper on Energy, when dealing with transportation fuels, may provide recommendations that indirectly influence the transportation sector. Such considerations could lead to an analysis of all other sectors' policy documents, having even the slightest potential impact on UFT. However, in order to define an accurate picture, the paper concentrates solely on the documents drafted by the European Directorate-General for Mobility and Transport (DG MOVE) of the European Commission and directly related to UFT[6]. In fact, since each DG has a key role in the definition of the H2020 affecting its sphere of influence, it is considered appropriate to assess the alignment between policy documents and H2020 calls produced by the same DG in the first place. The only exception is the Freight Transport Logistics Action Plan, since it specifically analyses UFT, delving into a significant aspect of logistics in general.

The third criterion simply assumes that only publicly available documents are considered.

Adopting the criteria illustrated above produces the list of documents reported below:

1. Transport White Paper 2001

2. Green Paper "Towards a new culture for urban mobility"

3. Freight transport logistics action plan

4. Action Plan on urban mobility

5. Transport White Paper 2011

6. Urban Mobility Package

7. A call to action on urban logistics

The second methodological step is the identification of the most important UFT policy solutions so to successively link them with H2020 Work Programmes. A qualitative analysis of the above-mentioned policy documents, investigating the entire set of relevant topics addressed, was carried out. An in-depth description is provided in section 3. The selection of the policy solutions is based on the following factors: i) how many, among the seven documents investigated, advocate these solutions (must be at least two), ii) the elements of continuity throughout all the seven documents, and iii) a qualitative assessment of the specific weight and degree of priority within each document.

The list of UFT solutions detected is reported here:

1. Including UFT in Sustainable Urban Mobility Plans (SUMPs) + guidelines for local authorities

2. Deployment of ITS systems for (urban) freight

3. Clean Freight vehicles

---

[5]Communications usually set out a Commission action plan and may include concrete proposals for legislation.

[6]Although many are the policy documents DG MOVE has published in the last 20 years, partly addressing urban mobility, this paper refers only to those explicitly dealing with UFT that are also listed on the DG move urban transport webpage: http://ec.europa.eu/transport/themes/urban/urban_mobility/index_en.htm

4. UFT demand management

5. eFreight

6. Integration between long-distance freight transport and last-mile distribution

7. Shift Modes (bike, boat, rail)

8. Integration between passenger and freight transport

9. Eco-labels

10. Public procurement for freight

The third step refers to the evaluation of the consistency between UFT priorities and H2020 funding. Firstly, a quantitative analysis of the "weight of freight" in the policy documents and H2020 Work Programmes is performed. As it is for the former, a matrix is produced counting the number of recurrences of the following words and combinations of them: i) urban ii) urban logistics; iii) city logistics; iv) urban freight; v) logistics; vi) freight; vii) passenger; viii) public transport. The logic behind the choice of these words is the following:

- "Urban": the paper narrows the scope of the analysis to the urban dimension of the goods distribution.

- "(urban/city) logistics" and "(urban) freight": according to a complete literature review, these are the most commonly used terms in the literature to refer to urban goods distribution.

- "Passengers" and "public transport": many studies (Lindholm 2010, Lindholm, Browne 2013, UN-Habitat 2013) have underlined the insufficient attention public authorities and European institutions pay to UFT operations. For various reasons, they seem to pay more attention to movements of people, rather than freight, i.e. undertaking policies for public transport and other passengers-related modes (Lindholm 2014). Therefore, the count of these words is used to compare the weight of the freight sector compared to the weight of the passenger sector in the European policy documents and H2020 Work Programmes.

This analysis indiscriminately considers how many times the specific words are mentioned in the documents, including titles, index and tables. A similar quantitative analysis is performed to provide an estimate of the weight urban logistics/freight topics hold in the H2020 programme considering the various calls, within "Mobility for Growth", directly or indirectly addressing UFT. The analysis is based on the calculation of the funding share actually allocated to UFT projects' proposals.

Finally, the paper both analyses the linkage between UFT policy solutions and H2020 Work Programmes and ranks the selected UFT policy solutions according to the weight, in monetary terms, resulting from the research funds allocated to each of them.

## 3 European strategy and UFT policy solutions

This section considers the seven policy documents listed in section 2, and highlights the policy priorities related to UFT, identifying ten corresponding solutions proposed by the European Commission.

The first European policy proposals in the area of urban mobility, the "Citizens' Network", date back to 1995 and 1998. They resulted in the launch of a series of initiatives based upon a "best practice" approach. However, the documents do not present any direct reference to UFT.

In 2001, the 1st White Paper on Transport was released (European Commission 2001). In Part 3 - Placing users at the heart of transport policy, section 4 specifically addresses the rationalisation of urban transport. The White Paper strategy for urban mobility essentially pursued two main objectives: 1) the promotion of a diversified energy portfolio for transport, by establishing a new regulatory framework for substitute and sustainable fuels and stimulating demand by experimentation; 2) the promotion and exchange of good practices, aiming at taking better use of public transport and existing infrastructure.

This White Paper didn't specifically address UFT. However, the CIVITAS initiative, launched in October 2000 to support the development of innovative projects on clean urban transport, represented an important step for research in this field, aiming at reducing private car use in city centres and promoting clean urban transport. The solutions envisaged went in three different directions: demand management measures, the integration of urban transport services, and the promotion of low and zero emissions vehicles, also for freight.

In 2007, a European policy document made explicit reference to UFT for the first time. In fact, the Green Paper "Towards a new culture for urban mobility" (European Commission 2007b) suggests local authorities to consider all urban logistics related to passenger and freight transport together as a single logistic system. Urban distribution needs for an efficient integration between long-distance freight transport and last mile distribution. To this end, the use of smaller, more efficient and clean vehicles is encouraged. When addressing UFT, local authorities should ensure the active involvement of all relevant stakeholders. UFT should be better integrated within the local policy-making process and institutional setting: freight transport distribution is often neglected and considered a mere responsibility of the private sector. Moreover, the role of intelligent transport systems (ITS) for freight becomes essential in order to improve efficiency, especially through better timing of operations, higher loading factors and more efficient use of vehicles. Finally, the document suggests (joint) green procurement of clean and energy-efficient vehicles by public authorities as a new solution to boost the deployment of clean vehicles.

The urban dimension of freight logistics is further developed in the Freight Transport Logistics Action Plan (European Commission 2007a). It reiterates that local authorities should focus their attention on transport demand management, supported by the deployment of innovative ITS-based solutions. In order for this to happen, a roadmap for the implementation of eFreight[7] should identify the critical areas where European actions are required (e.g. standardisation). The European Commission also commits to help establishing a set of recommendations, best practice and standards for urban transport logistics, aiming to define common benchmarks or performance indicators for the measurement of efficiency and sustainability of UFT solutions. This aims to reinforce the freight section of CIVITAS fostering the coordination and integration between passenger and freight transport, and between interurban (long-distance) and urban transport logistics.

Based upon the results of the consultation of the Green Paper, in 2009 the Action Plan on urban mobility was adopted (European Commission 2009), presenting for the first time a comprehensive support package of 20 measures in the field of urban mobility. This stresses again the importance of urban areas as efficient interconnection points for the trans-European transport network and places for a well-organised last mile transport. Action 1 introduces the concept of Sustainable Urban Mobility Plans, aiming to cover all types of transport, including UFT. Action 19 specifically addresses UFT, requiring to better incorporate it in the local transport strategy and to "better manage and monitor transport flows". Finally, the Plan aims to find new ways for improving and sharing data collection and statistics for urban transport and mobility (Actions 16 and 17).

In 2011, the 2nd White Paper on Transport was released (European Commission 2011). This document represents the current official position of the European Commission for transport in Europe, and sets a roadmap of 40 initiatives for the next decade to build a competitive transport system to increase mobility, foster growth and employment, reduce Europe's dependence on imported oil and cut carbon emissions in transport by 60% by 2050. It includes the specific objective of achieving "essentially CO2-free city logistics in major urban centres by 2030". The initiative n. 33, "a strategy for near-'zero-emission urban logistics' 2030", encourages again the realisation of best practice guidelines to "better monitor and manage urban freight flows", and promotes joint public procurement for low emission freight vehicles. Inspired by the above-mentioned Freight

---

[7]The concept of eFreight refers to the favouring of the multimodal transport of goods by creating the appropriate framework to allow tracing goods in real time and ensure intermodal liability.

Transport Logistics Action Plan, it claims a more efficient interface between long-distance and last-mile freight; the deployment of ITS for real-time traffic management, to increase efficiency for last mile distribution, and the definition of strategies for off-peak deliveries, to reduce air emissions and noise. The document also reinforces the concept of eFreight. The initiative n. 28, "vehicle labelling for CO2 emissions and fuel efficiency", launches a review of the labelling directive and also extends its scope to light freight vehicles.

The Urban Mobility Package (UMP) document (European Commission 2013b) promotes two non-regulatory initiatives related to the urban mobility sector. On the basis of the subsidiarity principle, it addresses initiatives 31, 32 and 33 of the 2011 White Paper. Initiative n. 33, as described before, refers to best practice guidelines to improve urban freight flows monitoring and management. The central element of the UMP is the Communication "Together towards competitive and resource-efficient urban mobility", complemented by an annex that sets out the concept of Sustainable Urban Mobility Plans (Wefering et al. 2013), as well as four Staff Working Documents (European Commission 2013a), one of which is dedicated to UFT. The central Communication, stressing the importance of the coordination between the public and private sector, claims the coordinated deployment of urban ITS and the importance of urban nodes, considered the "starting point or the final destination (first/last mile) for passengers and freight moving on the trans-European transport network". It fosters more action on UFT (aspect further developed in the Staff Working Document), promoting measures for the procurement of freight clean vehicles in the framework of the Clean Vehicle Portal[8]. It also defines the future scope of action of the CIVITAS initiative, which will focus on "tackling urban road congestion, reducing the use of conventionally-fuelled vehicles in urban areas, reducing UFT impacts and costs, and strengthening the capacities of local authorities to develop and implement sustainable urban mobility plans". All these topics directly or indirectly refer to UFT.

Finally, the most specific document on UFT is the "Call to action on urban logistics", Staff Working Document of the UMP. The document discusses the main challenges related to UFT and identifies possible solutions, also clarifying the role of each governance level (European, National, local) in the process. It highlights that the European research programmes have been supporting and will support research and dissemination for UFT vehicles and solutions, such as the CIVITAS projects. Some of them are focusing particularly on UFT, in testing innovative policy and technological solutions. As regards the challenges at stake, the document identifies e-commerce and online services; comprehensive UFT strategies for cities; cooperation and understanding amongst stakeholders; information and understanding of freight flows; information for urban transport operators about UFT policies, regulations and services; joint procurement of low emission urban freight vehicle; proper consideration of UFT in SUMPs. The solutions should follow four main directions: i) Manage urban logistic demand (service and delivery plans); ii) Shift modes (bike, boat or rail); iii) Improve efficiency (better selection of modes and vehicles, increasing load factors, new ITS solutions, eFreight initiatives, driver training); iv) Improved vehicles and fuels: new types of vehicles and operational models (e.g. electric vehicles, off-peak deliveries), deployment of alternative fuels infrastructure".

To sum up, the main policy solutions are summarised in Table 1.

## 4 Evaluation of policy priorities and funding

### 4.1 Quantitative analysis of the "weight of freight" in policy documents and H2020 Work Programmes

This sub-section reports the results of a quantitative analysis performed using the the seven selected policy documents and the two H2020 Work Programmes (2014-2015 and 2016-2017) published so far.

It is divided into two parts. The first provides a quantitative estimation of the "weight of freight" based on the number of recurrences of specific UFT-related words in the

---

[8]www.cleanvehicle.eu [27-08-2016 – offline]. The Clean Vehicle Portal as a new web-database aims to ensure a level of demand for clean and energy-efficient road transport vehicles and encourage manufacturers to invest in development of vehicles with low energy consumption CO2 emissions and pollutant emissions.

Table 1: Selected UFT policy solutions and their descriptions

| Policy Solution | Description |
| --- | --- |
| Including UFT in SUMPs + guidelines for local authorities | Member States should ensure UFT is given proper consideration in their national approaches to urban mobility and in SUMPs guidelines. Local authorities should include specific UFT provisions in their own SUMPs and enhance UFT stakeholder engagement in the planning/implementation process. |
| Deployment of ITS systems for (urban) freight | New ITS solutions can help to optimise routes, improve service and reduce costs and impacts. ITS allow for optimised trip planning, better traffic management and easier demand management. |
| Clean Freight vehicles | The operational characteristics of UFT can often be suitable for the early introduction of new types of vehicles (e.g. electric vehicles). Improvements in vehicles can make UFT quieter, safer, cleaner and more efficient. |
| UFT demand management | - new operational and business models: e.g. off-peak deliveries, reverse logistics, consolidation, increase load factors, logistic hotels, etc.<br>- incentives and regulations: parking policies, traffic and access regulations and charges, rewarding schemes, information and awareness raising. |
| eFreight | The concept of eFreight refers to the favouring of the multimodal transport of goods by creating the appropriate framework to allow tracing goods in real time and ensure intermodal liability. As part of the eFreight initiative, attention is given to the optimisation of information exchange for UFT as part of longer (international) logistics chains. |
| Integration between long-distance freight transport and last-mile distribution | Urban nodes are key elements for the construction of a comprehensive European transport network. Action by European cities is crucial for achieving the objectives of TEN-T policy. The European Commission recognises the need to "provide for the development of the comprehensive network in urban nodes, as those nodes are the starting point or the final destination ('last mile') for passengers and freight moving on the trans-European transport network and are points of transfer within or between different transport modes". |
| Shift Modes (bike, boat, rail) | Framework solutions provided by city authorities to create favourable conditions for freight shift modes, e.g. strategy, dedicated space, enforcement, privileged access, planning conditions, free parking etc., in order to achieve economic viability in addition to overall improvements. |
| Integration between passenger and freight transport | Local authorities need to consider all UFT related to passenger and freight transport together as a single logistics system. |
| Eco-labels | Introduction of a "labelling'" scheme to recognise the efforts of pioneering cities to combat congestion and improve living conditions. |
| Public procurement for freight | Support to projects and exchange of best practices to understand and facilitate joint procurement of urban freight vehicles and of public services and goods by public administrations. |

policy documents. The second part focuses on H2020 Work Programmes, illustrating the most relevant information linked to the calls specifically dealing with UFT providing an overview of the resources allocated to the various projects.

### 4.1.1 European policy documents

In order to support and reinforce the qualitative analysis performed in section 3 that enables selecting the main UFT-related policy solutions, a simple and straightforward quantitative approach is proposed here. The number of recurrences of specific UFT-related words have been systematically counted in the seven policy documents selected, so to provide a snapshot of the "weight of freight" for each of them.

In order to calculate the relative weight of UFT within the policy documents, the paper establishes a simple criterion: all the identified key words are standardised with respect to "urban" (last column in Table 2), which represents the minimum common denominator encompassing all the other ones. "Urban" is central in this analysis, since it represents the physical and conceptual dimension of both the freight and passenger transport sector policies at stake. In other words, the number of times "urban" is mentioned represents the "proxy" which allows us to quantify the relative "weight of freight".

Noticeably, in some cases and for single documents, the number of recurrences of some key words is higher than the number of recurrences of "urban" (in particular in Transport White Paper 2001 and Freight transport logistics action plan). This reflects the fact that those are broader documents addressing not only the "urban" dimension, but the whole transportation panorama in Europe. Therefore, key words such as "passengers" and "freight" quantitatively prevail, since they also refer to long-distance, extra-urban aspects of transportation.

The results of the quantitative analysis of the "weight of freight" in the policy documents is shown in Table 2 which reports, in absolute terms, the number of times given words or their combinations, directly or indirectly referring to UFT, appear in the documents considered.

As expected, the most frequently mentioned item is "urban" (547), followed by "freight" (241), while "logistics" (165) has fewer occurrences with respect to "passenger" (176). These items only partially address the specific topic considered in this paper. "Urban logistics" appears 72 times, whereas "urban freight" and "city logistics" 28 and 8 times, respectively, obtaining an overall result of 108 recurrences. It is interesting to note that most of the documents use both "urban logistics" and "city logistics", without explaining whether they are considered synonyms or different concepts. Moreover, an interesting result is that "passenger" and "public transport" occur, combined, the same number of times as "freight" (241). This result suggests a greater attention the freight sector has constantly gained among the European policy-makers over the last 20 years. However, when focusing the analysis at the urban level, the gap is still significant.

### 4.1.2 H2020 Work Programmes

H2020 is the European Research and Innovation programme, a source of nearly €80 billion[9] for European research activities for the 2014-2020 programming period. H2020 takes over the Seventh Framework Programme for Research and Technological Development (FP7)[10], and the Innovation section of the Competitiveness and Innovation Framework Programme (CIP).

The programme is based on three pillars: Excellent Science, Industrial Leadership and Social Challenges. The largest share of the budget (38.5%, €29.7 billion) is dedicated to the "Social challenges" pillar, which is, in turn, divided into seven thematic areas including "Smart, Green and Integrated Transport". A budget share of 8.2% (€6.3 billion) was allocated to the transport sector (Gavigan 2014). The challenge of H2020 is to create

---

[9] https://ec.europa.eu/programmes/horizon2020/en/what-horizon-2020

[10] FP7 was the main research programme for the 2007-2013 period, to give financial support to European initiatives promoting research, innovation and technological development for the creation of a European research area (ERA). With a budget of 50.521 billion euro, FP7 funded projects relating to research and technological development with the aim of stimulating growth, competitiveness and employment.

Table 2: Recurrences of UFT related words in the seven policy documents (absolute terms)

| Policy docs*<br>Key word(s) | 1 | 2 | 3 | 4 | 5 | 6 | 7 | Total | Weight wrt "urban" |
|---|---|---|---|---|---|---|---|---|---|
| Urban | 42 | 44 | 10 | 105 | 38 | 186 | 122 | 547 | - |
| City logistics | 0 | 0 | 0 | 0 | 2 | 2 | 4 | 8 | 1% |
| Urban logistics | 0 | 1 | 0 | 1 | 2 | 13 | 55 | 72 | 13% |
| Urban freight | 0 | 2 | 1 | 4 | 1 | 1 | 19 | 28 | 5% |
| Σ city logistics + urban logistics + urban freight | 0 | 3 | 1 | 5 | 5 | 16 | 78 | 108 | 19% |
| Logistics | 10 | 6 | 52 | 3 | 5 | 18 | 71 | 165 | 30% |
| Freight | 84 | 19 | 53 | 10 | 37 | 2 | 36 | 241 | 44% |
| Passenger | 110 | 20 | 2 | 10 | 32 | 1 | 1 | 176 | 32% |
| public transport | 32 | 13 | 0 | 12 | 5 | 3 | 0 | 65 | 12% |

*The documents taken into account are: 1) Transport White Paper 2001; 2) Green Paper "Towards a new culture for urban mobility"; 3) Freight transport logistics action plan;4) Action Plan on urban mobility; 5) Transport White Paper 2011; 6) Urban Mobility Package; 7) A call to action on urban logistics. *Source*: Self-elaboration

a transport system making efficient use of resources, which is environmentally friendly and safe. H2020 supports the research for new methods to obtain these results, and identifies two key topics, i) technology and ii) behavioural analysis, to develop innovative intervention strategies.

The budget is allocated every two years via a biannual Work Programme. Table 3 and Table 4 provide a budget overview of the H2020 Work Programmes 2014-2015 and 2016-2017, respectively, and an estimation of the (potential) financial support allocated for UFT in the framework of the "Mobility for Growth" call. With respect to FP7, the budget was increased by about 30%, considering the same topics (Gavigan 2014).

The first H2020 Work Programme (European Commission 2015a) was adopted on 10 December 2013 and structured in four broad cross-cutting lines of activities (i.e. resource efficient transport that respects the environment; better mobility, less congestion, more safety and security; global leadership for the European transport industry; socio-economic and behavioural research and forward looking activities for policy making) and three Calls for proposals (i.e. Mobility for Growth; Green Vehicles; Small Business Innovation for Transport) for an overall budget of €792.5 mln. Different calls for proposals directly or indirectly addressed UFT, but the call MG.5.2-2014 was specifically dedicated to this topic. In particular, it aimed at (i) improving basic knowledge and understanding on freight distribution and service trips, (ii) implementing innovative policies and solutions to ensure a better use of infrastructure (e.g. delivery spaces, off peak deliveries, non-road modes, urban waterways) and vehicles, (iii) testing consolidation and distribution centres. This call was directly linked to MG.6.1-2014 which looked for the right business models fostering (horizontal and vertical) synergies to decouple the growth of urban and inter-urban freight transport demand from its consequences on traffic and the environment. Other calls addressing UFT were MG.5.1-2014, MG.5.3-2014, MG.5.4-2015 and MG.5.5-2015. All of them generally referred to "freight", while the latter makes a specific reference to "urban freight logistics".

The Work Programme 2016-2017 was adopted on 13 October 2015, accompanied by an overall budget of €756.1 mln (European Commission 2015b). It presents the same structure and lines of activities of the previous one, with a small change in the calls for proposals. Again, in the urban mobility section there is a call dedicated to UFT, but in this case it addresses an even more specific topic. In fact, the title of the call is MG-4.3-2017 - Innovative approaches for integrating urban nodes in the TEN-T core network corridors. The solutions tested in this framework should investigate: (i)

Table 3: H2020 Work Programme 2014-2015: a budget overview

| Selected Call | | Budget (mln €) |
|---|---|---|
| *MG.5.1-2014* | *Transforming the use of conventionally fuelled vehicles in urban areas* | |
| MG.5.2-2014 | Reducing impacts and costs of freight and service trips | 40 |
| MG.5.3-2014 | Tackling urban road congestion | |
| MG.5.4-2015 | Strengthening the knowledge and capacities of local authorities | 9 |
| MG.5.5-2015 | Demonstrating and testing innovative solutions for cleaner and better urban transport and mobility | 57.5 |
| MG.6.1-2014 | Fostering synergies alongside the supply chain, including e-commerce | 32 |
| MG.6.2-2014 | De-stressing the supply chain | |
| *MG.7.1-2014* | *Connectivity and information sharing for intelligent mobility* | |
| *MG.7.2-2014* | *Towards seamless mobility addressing fragmentation in ITS deployment in Europe* | 28 |
| TOTAL (selected calls) | | 166.5 |
| Share of total funds allocated to calls to be potentially used for UFT projects | | (29.8%) |
| Total budget of Mobility for Growth calls [374.50 (2014) + 184 (2015)] | | 558.5 |

*Notes*: normal: calls *directly* addressing UFT; italic: calls *indirectly* addressing UFT

new approaches for linking long-distance with last-mile freight delivery in urban areas, (ii) the design of freight corridors in cities, (iii) an efficient and sustainable (e.g. using alternative fuel vehicles) solution for 'last mile' delivery, and a greater use of intermodal urban freight logistics. Nevertheless, other types of UFT innovative solutions can still be funded and tested through other urban mobility calls. In particular, the call MG-4.1-2017 includes issues such as new governance models for freight and passenger transport, better coordination and cooperation, synergies between passenger and freight transport, stakeholder engagement, etc. In the Logistics section, the first call MG-5.1-2016 is directly linked to MG-4.3-2017. In particular, it aims at connecting (sections of) the TEN-T freight network with each other and last mile delivery services, and developing prototype Modular Load Units, optimised for automated handling and high load factors in all transport modes. Although not directly related to UFT, the calls MG-5.2-2017 and MG-5.3-2016 pursue the deployment of ITS and green transport in the logistics sector. Other related calls are MG-4.2-2017 and MG-4.4-2016.

The total amount of funds allocated to the "Smart, Green and Integrated Transport" sector is €1,572.5 mln for the entire period 2014-2017. Out of this amount, the funds allocated to Mobility for Growth calls are €994.1 mln. According to the results shown in Tables 3 and 4, the share of the total funds allocated to calls that can be potentially addressed by UFT projects' proposals is €258.5 mln (26% of the total available budget), of which €166.5 mln (29.8% of the budget) for the period 2014-2015 and €92 mln (21.1% of the budget) for the period 2016-2017. This means that about a quarter of the total budget of the first 4 years of the H2020 programme is potentially available to fund UFT projects. Attention should be called to the difference in funding between the two periods: the first puts out a general call for UFT (MG.5.2-2014), and potentially allocates almost a third of the total funds to UFT projects; the second period proposes a very specific call for UFT (MG-4.3-2017) and potentially allocates only a fifth of the total funds to UFT projects.

As for the first period (2014-2015), the paper provides a further step of analysis. Since the funding period is over, it is possible to define the degree of alignment between the resources potentially available and the ones actually allocated (see Table 5). It may be noticed that 95% of the budget potentially available was actually assigned to projects (€157.4 vs €166.5 mln). Among these, considering the freight scope in general, a total of €57.5 mln has been allocated to thesetype of projects, corresponding to 36% of available

Table 4: H2020 Work Programme 2016-2017: a budget overview

| Selected Call | | Budget (mln €) |
|---|---|---|
| MG-4.4-2016 | *Facilitating public procurement of innovative sustainable transport and mobility solutions in urban areas* | 2 |
| MG-4.1-2017 | Increasing the take up and scale-up of innovative solutions to achieve sustainable mobility in urban areas | }22 |
| MG-4.2-2017 | Supporting 'smart electric mobility' in cities | |
| MG-4.3-2017 | Innovative approaches for integrating urban nodes in the TEN-T core network corridors | 2 |
| *MG-4.5-2016* | *New ways of supporting development and implementation of neighbourhood-level and urban-district-level transport innovations* | 10 |
| MG-5.1-2016 | Networked and efficient logistics clusters | 12 |
| MG-5.2-2017 | Innovative ICT solutions for future logistics operations | 12 |
| MG-5.3-2016 | Promoting the deployment of green transport, towards Eco-labels for logistics | 2 |
| *MG-6.2-2016* | *Large-scale demonstration(s) of cooperative ITS.* | 25[1] |
| MG-6.3-2016 | Roadmap, new business models, awareness raising, support and incentives for the roll-out of ITS | 5 |
| TOTAL (selected calls) | | 92 |
| Share of total funds allocated to calls to be potentially used for UFT projects | | (21.1%) |
| Total budget of Mobility for Growth calls [210.10 (2016) + 225.50 (2017)] | | 435.6 |

*Notes*: Key: normal: calls *directly* addressing UFT; *italic*: calls *indirectly* addressing UFT

[1] Unique budget for 6.1 & 6.2.

funds. Moreover, €31.7 mln have been specifically allocated to UFT projects[11]. This corresponds to 20% share of the overall available fund for the period 2014-2015.

Finally, a comparison between the relative "weight of freight", as outlined in Table 2, and the share of resources actually allocated to UFT projects, has been carried out. Results show an overall consistency: "city logistics", "urban logistics" and "urban freight" (considered as synonyms in this paper) are mentioned 19% of times with respect to "urban" (chosen as benchmarking) in the policy documents, the same percentage related to the funding share allocated to UFT projects. Similarly, "freight" is mentioned 44% of times with respect to "urban" in the policy documents, which is a percentage relatively close to the overall funding share of 36% attributed to freight projects. However, the picture changes when considering "logistics" as a synonym of "freight": in this case, the share rises up to 74%, significantly deviating from the share of funds actually attributed to freight projects.

## 4.2 Comparison between UFT solutions and corresponding call(s)

This section aims at analysing the link between the ten UFT policy solutions, considered essential for the achievement of a more efficient, less polluting and less impacting urban distribution of goods, and H2020 Work Programmes considering the weight in monetary terms resulting from the research funds allocated to each of them.

Table 6 shows the ten solutions, ranked according to the total funding budget available, along with the information about the documents where they are mentioned and the extent of their scope[12], indicating the corresponding H2020 calls in Work Programme 2014-15 and 2016-17.

The ten identified solutions differ in their scope: for example, "Including UFT in SUMPs" and "UFT demand management" can be defined in many different ways,

---

[11]UFT projects are those whose main objective is the adoption of sustainable solutions for UFT (for example, the SETRIS and PORTIS projects have a specific work package dedicated to UFT, but the main aim of the projects does not refer to this topic).

[12]The research qualitatively attributes a weight from 1 to 3, accordingly to the extent of the scope of each solution: + (narrow), ++ (medium), +++ (wide).

Table 5: Comparison between the resources potentially available and the ones actually allocated (Work Programme 2014-2015)

| Call | Acronym | European Union contribution (mln €) | Budget/call (mln €) |
|---|---|---|---|
| MG.5.1-2014 | EMPOWER | 4.9 | |
| | ELIPTIC | 6.0 | |
| MG.5.2-2014 | **SUCCESS** | 3.2 | |
| | **NOVELOG** | 4.4 | |
| | **CITYLAB** | 4.0 | |
| | **U-TURN** | 2.7 | |
| MG.5.3-2014 | CREATE | 4.0 | |
| | FLOW | 3.8 | |
| | TRACE | 2.9 | |
| | CIPTEC | 3.5 | |
| Subtotal (MG.5.1, 5.2, 5.3) | | 39.4 | 40 |
| MG.5.4-2015 | SUMPS-UP | 4.0 | |
| | PROSPERITY | 3.2 | |
| Subtotal (MG.5.4) | | 7.2 | 9 |
| MG.5.5-2015 | **CIVITAS ECCENTRIC** | 17.4 | |
| | CIVITAS DESTINATIONS | 17.9 | |
| | PORTIS | 16.4 | |
| | CIVITAS SATELLITE | 3.0 | |
| Subtotal (MG.5.5) | | 54.7 | 57.5 |
| MG.6.1-2014 | ***NEXTRUST*** | 18.1 | |
| MG.6.2-2014 | ***SYNCHRO-NET*** | 7.6 | |
| Subtotal (MG.6.1, 6.2) | | 25.7 | 32 |
| MG.7.1-2014 | SocialCar | 5.9 | |
| | OPTIMUM | 6.0 | |
| MG.7.2a-2014 | EuTravel | 3.9 | |
| | ETC | 4.5 | |
| | MASAI | 3.3 | |
| | BONVOYAGE | 4.0 | |
| MG.7.2b-2014 | ITS Observatory | 1.3 | |
| | CODECS | 1.6 | |
| Subtotal (MG.7.1, 7.2a, 7.2b) | | 30.5 | 28 |
| Total | | 157.5 | 166.5 |
| Total UFT projects | | 31.7 (20%) | |
| Total freight projects | | 57.4 (36%) | |
| Total non-freight projects | | 68.4 (64%) | |

*Key*: bold: UFT projects; bold&italic: freight projects

according to the specific topic the applicant wishes to address. Conversely, "eco labels" and "procurement" are specific enough and they can hardly be suitable for different interpretations. The results reported show that, in principle, each of the selected solutions is covered by at least one call.

Figure 1 summarises the information provided taking into account the following variables:

**1/a)** the extent of the scope of the solution that was normalised with respect to 7, which is the number of policy documents investigated;

**1/b)** number of policy documents addressing each solution according to the results of Table 6;

**2/a)** number of calls considering each solution, as reported in Table 6. The maximum number of calls for a given solution is 7, thus normalisation is not needed;

**2/b)** budget (potentially) available for each solution. Directly linked to the calls, the amount per solution, specified in Table 6, is normalised with respect to 7.

In general, 2/a and 2/b follow the same steady decreasing trend, highlighting the consistency between the amount of funds and the related calls that make them available.1/a and 1/b both follow a more volatile path, nevertheless presenting the same fluctuations and a decreasing trend which is overall consistent with the one of 2/a and 2/b.

Four of the UFT solutions present an overall consistency when it comes to comparing 1/a) and 1/b), on the one hand, and 2/a) and 2/b), on the other: the greater (lesser) the scope of the solution and the higher (lower) the number of mentions in policy documents, the more (less) it is addressed in H2020 calls and, therefore, more (less) potential budget available for its implementation. This seems the case for "UFT in SUMPs", "clean freight vehicles", "shift modes", "integration passenger/freight".

There are five solutions, out of ten, which do not present a clear path: "UFT demand management", "eco-labels" and "public procurement for freight" seem under-funded (or over-covered), whereas "eFreight" and "ITS", on the contrary, seems over-funded (or under-covered).

These solutions are discussed in more detail in what follows. In recent years, transport demand management has been discovered to influence agents' behaviour in the urban sector (e.g. Ben-Elia, Avineri 2015, Dziekan, Kottenhoff 2007, Juhász 2013, Marcucci et al. 2007, 2013a,b, Mokhtarian, Salomon 2001, Watkins et al. 2011), through the adoption of soft policy measures (SPMs). These are gaining increasing attention in the field of sustainable mobility for various reasons, such as the lack of large budgets available or public dissent against coercive measures (Gärling, Schuitema 2007). SPMs aim to influence transport actors' mobility choices, and therefore altering the demand for mobility (Jones et al. 2011). SPMs are often low-cost, compared to the other solutions, making "UFT demand management" a very cost-effective approach. In fact, it does not require a significant financial investment for research and innovation, but rather an extensive investigation on how the implementation and exchange of UFT SPMs' best practices can be spread to ensure it is raising awareness and successfully transferring and adapting to different contexts. It is important to note that a robust demand analysis should foresee an evaluation of stakeholders' policy acceptability, behaviour change and willingness to pay measures (e.g. Gatta et al. 2015, Le Pira et al. 2017b, Marcucci, Gatta 2016). Recent trends in freight demand management includes: i) off-hour deliveries (e.g. Holguín-Veras et al. 2014, Marcucci, Gatta 2017); ii) crowdshipping (e.g. Marcucci et al. 2017c, Punel, Stathopoulos 2017).

"Public procurement for freight" and "eco-labels" are also an effective and relatively low-cost solution and, in some respects, they follow the same principles as the "UFT demand management" category: the use of the procurement leverage and recognition schemes (including eco-labelling) potentially enhance safety and reduce emissions. Indeed, public administrations might set rules to procure external services according to certain "green" standards. In this way, they i) give signals to UFT stakeholders to improve their sustainability standards in order to participate in public tenders, and ii) give an example

Table 6: Comparison between UFT solutions and corresponding call(s)

| UFT solutions[1] | Corresponding call(s)[2] | Budget available[3] |
| --- | --- | --- |
| **1) Including UFT in SUMPs + guidelines for local authorities (focus on stakeholder engagement)** Policy documents: 2, 3, 4, 6, 7 Extent of the scope of the solution: +++ | MG.5.2-2014 | *13* |
| | MG.5.4-2015 | 9 |
| | MG.5.5-2015 | 57.5 |
| | MG-4.1-2017 | *22* |
| | MG-4.2-2017 | |
| | MG-4.3-2017 | 2 |
| | **Total** | **103.5** |
| **2) Deployment of ITS systems for (urban) freight** Policy documents: 2, 3, 5, 6, 7 Extent of the scope of the solution: ++ | MG.6.1-2014 | *16* |
| | *MG.7.1-2014* | 28 |
| | *MG.7.2-2014* | 28 |
| | MG-6.2-2016 | *12.5* |
| | MG-6.3-2016 | 5 |
| | *MG-4.2-2017* | *11* |
| | MG-5.2-2017 | 12 |
| | **Total** | **84.5** |
| **3) Clean Freight vehicles** Policy documents: 1, 2, *4*, 5, 6, 7 Extent of the scope of the solution: ++ | *MG.5.1-2014* | *13* |
| | GV.4-2014 | *18* |
| | *MG-4.2-2017* | *11* |
| | GV-08-2017 | *16* |
| | **Total** | **58** |
| **4) UFT demand management** Policy documents: 1, 3, *4, 5, 6*, 7 Extent of the scope of the solution: +++ | MG.5.2-2014 | *26* |
| | MG.5.3-2014 | |
| | MG.6.1-2014 | *16* |
| | MG-4.1-2017 | *11* |
| | MG-4.3-2017 | 2 |
| | **Total** | **55** |
| **5) eFreight** Policy documents: 5, 7 Extent of the scope of the solution: + | *MG.6.1-2014* | 32 |
| | MG.6.2-2014 | |
| | MG-5.2-2017 | 12 |
| | *MG-4.2-2017* | *11* |
| | **Total** | **55** |
| **6) Integration between long-distance freight transport and last-mile distribution** Policy documents: 2, 3, 4, 5, 6 Extent of the scope of the solution: ++ | MG.6.1-2014 | *16* |
| | MG-4.3-2017 | 2 |
| | MG-5.1-2016 | *13* |
| | **Total** | **31** |
| **7) Shift Modes (bike, boat, rail)** Policy documents: *1*, 7 Extent of the scope of the solution: + | MG.5.2-2014 | 26 |
| | MG.5.3-2014 | |
| **8) Integration between passenger and freight transport** Policy documents: 2, 3 Extent of the scope of the solution: + | MG-4.1-2017 | *11* |
| | *MG-4.5-2016* | 10 |
| | **Total** | **21** |
| **9) Eco-labels** Policy documents: 2, 5 Extent of the scope of the solution: + | MG-5.3-2016 | **2** |
| **10) Public procurement for freight** Policy documents: 2, 5, 6, 7 Extent of the scope of the solution: + | MG-4.4-2016 | **2** |

[1] normal: policy documents directly mentioning the selected solution; *italic*: policy documents indirectly mentioning the selected solution. Extent of the scope of the solution (qualitative assessment) from + to +++. Policy documents: 1= Transport White Paper 2001; 2= Green Paper; 3= Freight transport logistics action plan; 4= Action Plan on urban mobility; 5= Transport White Paper 2011; 6= Urban Mobility Package; 7= A call to action on urban logistics
[2] normal: calls directly addressing the solution; *italic*: calls indirectly addressing the solution.
[3] *italic*: estimated budget in the case more calls are grouped under a unique budget item

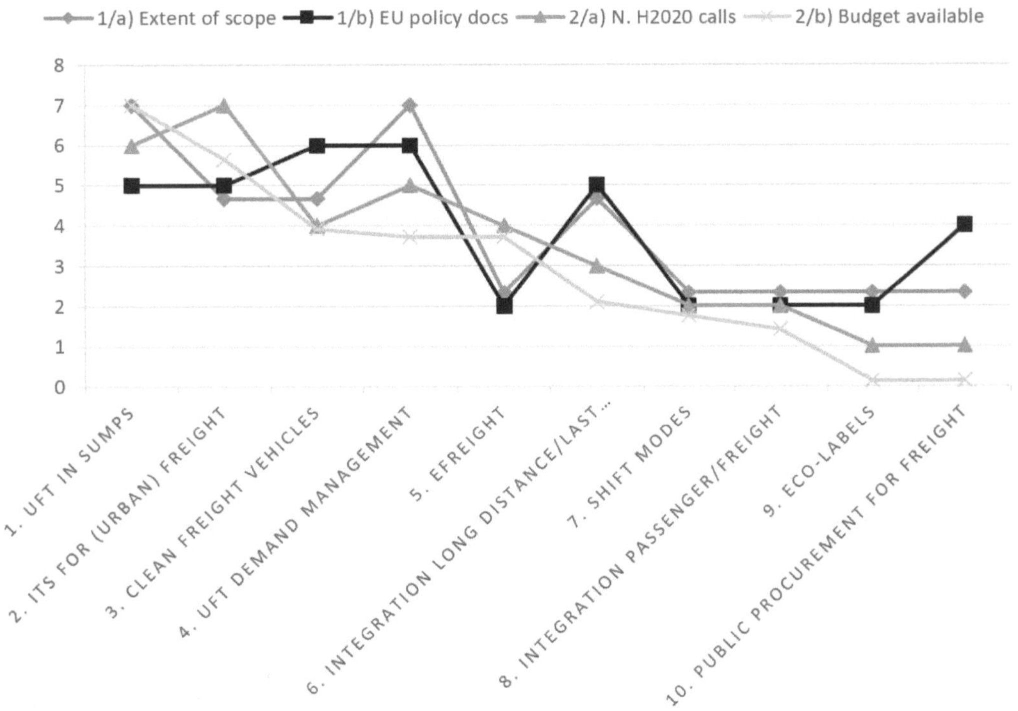


Figure 1: Analysis of the selected UFT policy solutions

of good practice, triggering a virtuous circle that allows them to frame these choices in the framework of behaviour change campaigns.

"eFreight", mentioned in four calls, obtains an average ranking position, and "Deployment of ITS systems for (urban) freight" is also present in many documents. They can be addressed in many different calls, but only some of them specifically refer to UFT, affecting the possibility that a UFT-related project gets funded, because of the strong competition of other non-UFT-related project proposals.

To conclude, unlike other solutions, "Integration between long-distance freight transport and last-mile distribution", is cited in almost all the documents but is considered only in few and very specific calls. This apparently biased result can be explained by the intrinsic characteristics this solution has, requiring more implementation than research supporting activities. In this case, other types of funding instruments which are not considered in this paper (e.g. Connecting Europe Facility[13] funds which finance the trans-European transport network projects[14]) seem more appropriate.

## 5  Discussion and conclusions

The paper proposes an innovative approach for the assessment of the coherence and consistency between policy priorities and funds allocated to related research activities. It provides a systematic (living) "matching" tool, capable of constantly monitoring the parallel evolution of policies and projects.

Firstly, the paper carries out a detailed analysis identifying the UFT challenges, and the related policy solutions defined at European level. Findings show that, starting from 2001, with the 1st White Paper on Transport, and, in a more comprehensive way, from 2007, with the Green Paper, the European Commission addresses UFT challenges

---

[13]The Connecting Europe Facility for Transport is the funding instrument to realise European transport infrastructure policy. It aims at supporting investments in building new transport infrastructure in Europe or rehabilitating and upgrading the existing one.

[14]Since 2014, some Connecting Europe Facility calls address the urban nodes i.e. the cities on the network. Over 2014-2015, up to €500 million were dedicated to urban nodes.

through a systematic and coherent approach. Most of the significant priorities (constantly updated) aim to reach the same long-term objectives. Moreover, in 2013 the European Commission decided to dedicate one of the four accompanying documents of the Urban Mobility package to UFT ("A call to action on urban logistics"). This testifies the growing attention conferred to this topic. Ten solutions are proposed for the achievement of a more efficient, less polluting and less impacting urban distribution of goods.

At a second stage, the paper illustrates the H2020 research programme, providing an overview of the total budget allocated to it and the share of funds allocated to the transport sector. Based on the main UFT priorities identified in the policy documents, the paper selects the corresponding calls from the 2014-2015 and 2016-2017 H2020 Work Programmes to quantify the funds available to (potentially) finance UFT projects. The total amount of funds allocated to the "Smart, Green and Integrated Transport" sector is €1,572.5 mln for the period 2014-2017. About a quarter of the total budget of the first 4 years of the programme is potentially available to finance UFT projects, which represents a satisfactory share of available funds. The paper also investigates, limited to the concluded funding period 2014-2015, whether and how the funds a priori allocated correspond to those actually credited. Encouraging results are found. In fact, €31.8 mln are allocated to UFT projects, representing a 20% share of the overall potentially available funds. Moreover, considering the "freight scope" in general, a total of €57.4 mln are allocated, representing a 36% share of the available funds. These findings show an overall consistency with the "weight of freight" index. In fact, "city logistics", "urban logistics" and "urban freight" hold together a relative weight of 19% in the policy documents, almost the same percentage of funds attributed to UFT projects (20%). "Freight" holds a relative weight of 44% in the policy documents, again close to an overall funding share of 36% of freight-related projects.

The approach proposed gives the opportunity to "weight" the importance of all significant UFT solutions proposed, by tying them with the H2020 Work Programmes and the corresponding budget allocated for their development and deployment. Results show that each of the selected solutions is covered by at least one call. As a consequence, there is the opportunity to undertake research and innovation projects in each of the UFT priority areas. Four of the UFT solutions present an overall consistency when it comes to comparing the extent of the scope of the solution and the number of documents addressing it, on the one hand, and the number of calls considering it and the budget (potentially) available, on the other. Other solutions do not follow a clear path. "UFT demand management" policies, "eco-labels" and "public procurement" can be considered cost-effective solutions, not requiring a significant financial investment. According to these findings, future research should identify the most promising UFT SPMs in the field of "UFT demand management", implying a behaviour changing approach, and consequently test their potential for rolling out to different local environments. This also implies a higher level of local UFT stakeholders' involvement and cooperation, led by local authorities (Lindholm, Browne 2013, Marcucci et al. 2017b, Quak et al. 2015), which can materialise into cooperative schemes, incentives and public-private partnerships. Indeed, recent literature indicates the need for including stakeholders' preferences and their interactions within a participatory planning process (Gatta et al. 2017, Le Pira et al. 2017a, Marcucci et al. 2017a).

Looking at the list of the ten priorities identified in the policy documents, it is evident there is an absence of data collection and modelling for UFT. Data collection and modelling are essential to observe and analyse the movements of goods in urban areas in a reliable and comparable way, and, consequently, to plan and implement solutions based on the real needs of each context.

The need to place greater emphasis on research in this sector is also highlighted in the aforementioned Urban Freight Roadmap of ALICE/ERTRAC (2014), which "identifies data collection and knowledge building for urban logistics as the first step for a relevant urban logistics research agenda". It also considers that the "development and use of modeling tools is necessary to better understand the economics and behaviour and assess the impact of (...) policy measures".

The H2020 call MG.5.2-2014 (see section 4.1.2) has partially addressed this issue, promoting research on indicators, measurement and data, as well as economic and behavioral modelling. However, the related projects have not been sufficiently coordinated in terms of sharing and consolidation of results, as would be appropriate for such a topic: it is emblematic of the non-binding guidelines of the European Commission "Data collection methodologies for urban freight policy", meant to provide specific information on the data that can be collected, purposes and best practices. Initially scheduled for January 2017, they have not yet been published. Therefore, further effort is still needed to develop a clearer and stronger strategy regarding research on new methods and practices for data collection and modelling.

To sum up, over the past 20 years, the identified challenges and the proposed solutions are developed in a consistent manner and UFT is sufficiently covered by H2020 research funds. However, funds are heterogeneously allocated between the UFT policy solutions investigated. It should be borne in mind that the research funds allocated by the H2020 Work Programmes are specifically intended for research projects. The paper does not investigate other funding, in particular the structural funding, nor other related European programmes, such as the Connecting Europe Facility for Transport, created for the implementation of the identified solutions, in particular as regards infrastructure improvements.

Future endeavours could imply extending the research to other DGs, policy documents and European funds, to understand and evaluate how the urban transport sector policy fits with and is affected by the overall European policies in terms of environment, energy, growth, competition, regionalism, etc. This will require a fully dedicated new study, since details and a complete coverage of European non-binding instruments addressing urban transport is difficult to obtain and incomplete, and the amount of those is likely to be very high.

## References


ALICE/ERTRAC (2014) Urban freight research roadmap. Retrieved from: http://www.ertrac.org/uploads/documentsearch/id36/ERTRAC˙Alice˙Urban˙Freight.pdf

Ben-Elia E, Avineri E (2015) Response to travel information: A behavioural review. *Transport Reviews* 35[3]: 999–999. CrossRef.

Dziekan K, Kottenhoff K (2007) Dynamic at-stop real-time information displays for public transport: effects on customers. *Transportation Research Part A Policy and Practice* 41[6]: 489–501. CrossRef.

European Commission (2001) European transport policy for 2010: time to decide. Transport White Paper. COM(2001) 370

European Commission (2007a) Freight transport logistics action plan. COM(2007) 607 final

European Commission (2007b) Towards a new culture for urban mobility. Transport Green Paper. COM(2007) 551 final

European Commission (2009) Action plan on urban mobility. COM(2009) 490

European Commission (2011) Roadmap to a single European transport area – Towards a competitive and resource efficient transport system. Transport White paper. COM(2011) 144 final

European Commission (2013a) A call to action on urban logistics. SWD(2013) 524 final

European Commission (2013b) Urban mobility package. COM(2013) 913 final

European Commission (2015a) 11. smart, green and integrated transport. Horizon 2020 Work Programme 2014 - 2015 (Revised). Decision C (2015)2453 of 17 April 2015

European Commission (2015b) 11. smart, green and integrated transport. Horizon 2020 Work Programme 2016 - 2017 (Revised). Decision C (2015)6776 of 13 October 2015)

Gatta V, Marcucci E, Le Pira M (2017) Smart urban freight planning process: integrating desk, living lab and modelling approaches in decision-making. *European Transport Research Review* 9: 32. CrossRef.

Gatta V, Marcucci E, Scaccia L (2015) On finite sample performance of confidence intervals methods for willingness to pay measures. *Transportation Research Part A: Policy and Practice* 82: 169–192. CrossRef.

Gavigan J (2014) Horizon 2020 – the EU framework programme for research and innovation 2014-2020. Ppt presentation at the european union delegation to the usa, november 2014. available at https://ec.europa.eu/research/iscp/pdf/sanjose-2015/H2020.pdf

Gärling T, Schuitema G (2007) Travel demand management targeting reduced private car use: effectiveness, public acceptability and political feasibility. *Journal of Social Issues* 63: 139–153. CrossRef.

Holguín-Veras J, Wang C, Browne M, Darville Hodge S, Wojtowicz J (2014) The New York City off-hour delivery project: lessons for city logistics. *Procedia – Social and Behavioral Sciences* 125: 36–48. CrossRef.

Jones R, Pykett J, Whitehead M (2011) Governing temptation: changing behaviour in an age of libertarian paternalism. *Progress in Human Geography* 35[4]: 483–501. CrossRef.

Juhász M (2013) Travel demand management – possibilities of influencing travel behaviour. *Periodica Polytechnica, Transportation Engineering* 41[1]: 45–50. CrossRef.

Le Pira M, Marcucci E, Gatta V, Ignaccolo M, Inturri G, Pluchino A (2017a) Towards a decision-support procedure to foster stakeholder involvement and acceptability of urban freight transport policies. *European Transport Research Review* 9: 54. CrossRef.

Le Pira M, Marcucci E, Gatta V, Inturri G, Ignaccolo M, Pluchino A (2017b) Integrating discrete choice models and agent-based models for ex-ante evaluation of stakeholder policy acceptability in urban freight transport. *Research in transportation economics* 64: 13–25

Lindholm M (2010) A sustainable perspective on urban freight transport: Factors affecting local authorities in the planning procedures. *Procedia – Social and Behavioral Sciences* 2[3]: 6205–6216. CrossRef.

Lindholm M (2014) Successes and failings of an urban freight quality partnership – The story of the Gothenburg local freight network. *Procedia – Social and Behavioral Sciences* 125: 125–135. CrossRef.

Lindholm M, Browne M (2013) Local authority cooperation with urban freight stakeholders: A comparison of partnership approaches. *European Journal of Transport and Infrastructure Research* 13[1]: 20–38

Marcucci E, Danielis R, Paglione G, Gatta V (2007) Centri urbani di distribuzione delle merci e politiche del traffico: una valutazione empirica tramite le preferenze dichiarate. Atti del 7 congresso ciriaf, 373-378

Marcucci E, Gatta V (2016) How good are retailers in predicting transport providers' preferences for urban freight policies? ...and vice versa? *Transportation Research Procedia* 12: 193–202. CrossRef.

Marcucci E, Gatta V (2017) Investigating the potential for off-hour deliveries in the city of Rome: Retailers' perceptions and stated reactions. *Transportation Research Part A: Policy and Practice* 102: 142–156. CrossRef.

Marcucci E, Gatta V, Marciani M, Cossu P (2017b) Measuring the effects of an urban freight policy package defined via a collaborative governance model. *Research in Transportation Economics* 65: 3–9. CrossRef.

Marcucci E, Gatta V, Stathopoulos A, Valeri E (2013a) Urban freight policy acceptability: eliciting agent specific preferences via efficient experimental design. *Zeitschrift für Verkehrswissenschaft* 3: 237–259

Marcucci E, Gatta V, Valeri E, Stathopoulos A (2013b) *Urban freight transport modelling: an agent-specific approach.* Franco Angeli, Milano

Marcucci E, Le Pira M, Carrocci CS, Gatta V, Pieralice E (2017c) Connected shared mobility for passengers and freight: Investigating the potential of crowdshipping in urban areas. 5th IEEE International Conference on Models and Technologies for Intelligent Transportation Systems (MT-ITS), 839-843

Marcucci E, Le Pira M, Gatta V, Ignaccolo M, Inturri G, Pluchino A (2017a) Simulating participatory urban freight transport policy-making: Accounting for heterogeneous stakeholders' preferences and interaction effects. *Transportation Research Part E* 103: 69–86

MDS – MDS Transmodal Limited (2012) European commission: Study on urban freight transport. DG MOVE final report. Available at http://ec.europa.eu/transport/themes/-urban/studies/doc/2012-04-urban-freight-transport.pdf

Mokhtarian PL, Salomon I (2001) How derived is the demand for travel? Some conceptual and measurement considerations. *Transportation research part A: Policy and practice* 35[8]: 695–719. CrossRef.

Punel A, Stathopoulos A (2017) Modeling the acceptability of crowdsourced goods deliveries: Role of context and experience effects. *Transportation Research Part E: Logistics and Transportation Review* 105: 18 38. CrossRef.

Quak H, Lindholm M, Tavasszy L, Browne M (2015) From freight partnerships to city logistics living labs – giving meaning to the elusive concept of living labs. 9th International Conference on City Logistics, Tenerife, Spain, 17-19 June

UN-Habitat (2013) Planning and design for sustainable urban mobility. Global report on human settlements 2013. available at https://unhabitat.org/planning-and-design-for-sustainable-urban-mobility-global-report-on-human-settlements-2013/

Watkins KE, Ferris B, Borning A, Scott Rutherford G, Layton D (2011) Where is my bus? impact of mobile real-time information on the perceived and actual wait time of transit riders. *Transportation Research Part A: Policy and Practice* 45[8]: 839–848. CrossRef.

Wefering F, Rupprecht S, Bührmann S, Böhler-Baedeker S (2013) Guidelines. developing and implementing a sustainable urban mobility plan. Rupprecht consult

The Journal of ERSA
Powered by WU

Volume 4, Number 1, 2017, 93–107
DOI: 10.18335/region.v4i1.158

journal homepage: region.ersa.org

# Logistics sprawl in monocentric and polycentric metropolitan areas: the cases of Paris, France, and the Randstad, the Netherlands

Adeline Heitz[1], Laetitia Dablanc[2], Lorant A. Tavasszy[3]

[1] University of Paris East, Paris, France (email: adeline.heitz@ifsttar.fr)
[2] IFSTTAR, Paris, France (email: laetitia.dablanc@ifsttar.fr)
[3] Delft University of Technology, Delft, The Netherlands (email: l.a.tavasszy@tudelft.nl)

Received: 5 September 2016/Accepted: 13 April 2017

**Abstract.** The phenomenon of urban sprawl has been studied extensively. Most research so far has focused on residential settlements. A growing number of studies have addressed industrial deconcentration. Our focus in this paper is on logistics sprawl, i.e. the growth and suburban relocation of warehousing activities. Specifically, we investigate the difference in logistics sprawl between monocentric and polycentric systems of cities. The literature suggests that logistics activities, like residential settlements, will gradually move to suburbs as land prices increase in central areas. As research on logistics geography has mostly focused on monocentric systems, the question is whether this also applies to polycentric systems. We compare two cases, the Paris region in France, representative of a monocentric urban development, and the Dutch Randstad area as a polycentric case. We use regional statistics on warehouse settlements in both regions for a descriptive analysis of changes since the mid-2000s to derive metrics for concentration. The cases show different patterns of change. In contrast to Paris, logistics activities within the Randstad have intensified in dense areas. We explore the reasons that may explain this difference and conclude that urban structure, spatial planning policies, and the freight hub quality of a region are factors of influence.

## 1 Introduction

The recent growth of logistics activities including warehousing has increased their importance in metropolitan areas (Bowen 2008). Logistics activities are sprawling outwards and warehouses are leaving dense areas and relocating in peripheral ones. Logistics sprawl is the subject of a growing volume of research. North American metropolitan areas such as Chicago (Cidell 2010), Atlanta (Dablanc, Ross 2012) or Toronto (Woudsma et al. 2015) have been covered by pioneering work on logistics sprawl. Several studies have examined the case of Paris (Dablanc, Rakotonarivo 2010, Raimbault, Bahoken 2014). With the exception of Paris there have been few case studies in Europe.

Yet European metropolitan areas, far from forming a homogeneous whole, are characterized by long-established and variable urban forms. The literature (see below) distinguishes between two main types of urban region structure: monocentric and polycentric, which are actually the two extremes of a continuum of urban regions. Europe has a large number of monocentric urban regions such as Paris or London, but also polycentric urban regions like the Randstad region (Davoudi 2003). Polycentric and monocentric urban regions each provide a specific urban context for the development of economic activities. Monocentric urban regions are characterized by their large and growing population and the fact that economic and leadership activities are concentrated in one metropolitan area. These factors mean that they also have a considerable capacity for growth, so, in spatial terms, they expand physically. The dense, uninterrupted, parts of a large city are easily identifiable. However, urbanized areas of its outer suburbs, which are scattered over distances of several tens of kilometers from the center, are difficult to distinguish from rural areas. The urban area includes the central conurbation and its suburban rings, which itself contain secondary centers of various sizes. This urban region has the appearance of a "macroform" (Allain 2004). Polycentric urban regions are, on the opposite, made of several urban centers, which polarize population and activities, and which are linked to each other by flows (freight, people, information) and cooperation or interdependent bounds of various types. Cities within a polycentric urban region seem to have merged in a functional and morphological entity: a large and dispersed regional urban system. Polycentric regions are characterized by the fact that residential and economic functions are distributed within the metropolis between clearly separated specialized centers of employment (Berroir et al. 2008). The residential function is organized around these centers, forming high-density clusters.

In this paper, we examine the impact of the metropolitan structure on the development of logistics spatial dynamics. We have chosen two archetypal urban regions, Paris and the Randstad, in order to take a different view on the location's factors traditionally observed in the literature. By using the same method and the same kind of data for both areas, we want to contribute to the general debate on the location's factors for logistics facilities. By observing the evolution of the location of logistics facilities in metropolitan areas which are located either in a monocentric urban region or in a polycentric urban region, we want to test the recurrence of the logistics deconcentration and learn from potential differences. This paper also contributes to establishing the distinction between "logistics sprawl" and "logistics suburbanization".

The remainder of the paper is built up as follows. Section 2 provides a literature review on logistics deconcentration, logistics sprawl and the main drivers that usually explain this dynamic. Section 3 explains the data used for the analysis and the results of the comparison of the two regions and provides an interpretation of the results regarding contrasting forms of logistics urbanization in the two regions. Section 4 provides an analysis of new drivers explaining the deconcentration process in those metropolitan areas, including public policies and their potential impact on logistics spatial patterns. We conclude the paper in Section 5.

## 2 Logistics sprawl and logistics suburbanization

### 2.1 Logistics sprawl in metropolitan areas: a state of the art

Over the last thirty years, a process of metropolization has further increased urban growth and urban sprawl. Metropolitan areas have spread out because of a lack of available space in the dense parts of the conurbation (Nicot 1996) to accommodate this growth. Urban deconcentration is the outcome of the gradual saturation of the most central areas and increases in the price of land because of its relative scarcity. Logistics deconcentration, or sprawl, means an increasing number of logistics facilities in peripheral areas and their dispersion. It describes the decreasing number of logistics activities, such as warehouses, in urban centers, and their redistribution in the periphery. This is what is known as "centrifugal growth" in the typology developed by Champion (2001). What occurs is that secondary centers emerge in peripheral areas where property prices and traffic congestion are lower. These secondary centers are easily accessible thanks to high speed transport infrastructure. According to the typology developed by Le Nechet, Aguiléra (2012), Paris is a type of "pyramid" metropolis, that is to say an isotropic space in which land market forces theoretically lead to an exponential decrease in population density with distance from the employment center.

Several factors explain logistics sprawl. First, the nature of supply chain management has shifted concomitantly from "supply-push" to "demand-pull" systems (Lasserre 2004).

In the former, firms "pushed" their output into distribution channels based on demand forecasts, relying on storage places close to production sites. In the latter, firms gear their production in response to real-time information about what consumers are buying, and use distribution centers closer to consumer markets (Bowen 2008). Changes in supply chain management impacted the location of logistics facilities. Moreover, historically, the majority of these storage buildings were smaller and located in inner urban areas in the proximity of industrial areas, rail terminals, and docklands (Dablanc, Rakotonarivo 2010, Cidell 2010). Changes in the location of transportation terminals also influenced the location. Because of an increasing size of facilities, large and cheap available land parcels were more likely found in suburbs and exurbs.

In a recent literature review paper, Aljohania, Thompson (2016) identifies studies showing that "land use control and the exclusion of freight in urban planning have influenced a relocation of logistics facilities from inner urban areas to suburban areas, as affordable industrial land was no longer available for logistics companies". Nicot (1996) concludes that the lack of industrial land in inner urban areas is a primary driver in the relocation of logistics facilities away from urban cores. Merenne-Schoumaker (2008) identifies several indicators that guide the choice of location of logistics activities and warehousing establishments. First of all, land availability appears to be decisive. Distribution centers tend to require fewer and larger single-story facilities from 10,000 to 100,000 m2 ("XXL warehouses") (Hesse 2004, Cidell 2010). Consequently, suburban and exurban areas offer more affordable locations for logistics facilities. In a monocentric urban area, the price of land decreases from the center of the metropolitan area to the periphery. In polycentric urban areas, the price of land decreases for each center to each periphery, but the decrease is limited by the proximity to each metropolitan area. Suburban areas appear to be favored land for logistics facilities' development. In order to compensate for the remoteness, logistics facilities rely on accessibility and choose to locate close to the main roads and highways, which ensure access to labor markets and consumption areas. The last factor of location, identified by Merenne-Schoumaker and also underlined by Aljohania, Thompson (2016), is the role of public policies in land use. By regulating, funding, or planning dedicated zones for logistics, public policies encourage the location of logistics facilities in determined areas. The location of logistics facilities is not only driven by market forces and land opportunities.

### 2.2 From logistics sprawl to logistics suburbanization

Land availability appears to be decisive. Consequently, suburban and exurban areas offer more affordable locations for logistics facilities. Suburban areas appear to be favored land for logistics facilities' development. In the case of the Paris region, Dablanc, Rakotonarivo (2010) showed that the parcel industry has moved to the periphery as a result of centrifugal forces. Paris infrastructure heritage initially favored the concentration of logistics and freight transport in dense central areas. Then some of these logistics activities, including distribution centers (Raimbault 2015), were transferred to peripheral areas.

In this paper, we make a distinction between 'logistics sprawl' and 'logistics suburbanization.' Logistics suburbanization has an additional qualitative meaning to the mere relative increase in the number of warehouses in areas further away from the city center. Logistics suburbanization describes the transformation of low density suburbs and the irruption/integration of logistics in the outskirts of the metropolitan area. Suburbanization can be defined as the urbanization of peripheral areas (generally with low density settlements). Spaces with lower densities provide the most attractive location for these warehouses, especially as modern warehouses are larger and in requirement of large land parcels. This development of logistics in the outskirts not only contributes to the expansion of metropolitan areas, but also reshapes the suburban areas that accommodate such activities. Logistics suburbanization corresponds to a "third phase" of logistics development (Frémont 2015). Logistics functions are discharged to external centers in the urban periphery where available space for large warehouses can meet current demand. This may present a problem not only for their spatial optimization but also for land use efficiency. Indeed, the development of logistics areas in the metropolitan fringes can promote a process of urban disintegration (Hall, Hesse 2013).

Logistics suburbanization depends on/results in a high level of goods transport. The concentration of logistics activities in the suburbs redefines the functions of both dense and suburban areas. Suburban areas become supporting territories, bases or intermediate points for the flow of goods, and often the last place before the final distribution of goods. The relationship between central and peripheral areas is linked to the flow of goods from a suburban warehouse into dense city areas.

Hall, Hesse (2013) pointed out in the conclusion of their study that the deconcentration of logistics activities as a suburban development is a "surprisingly common" phenomenon in many cities, presenting a challenge for public authorities. It seems appropriate to put this conclusion into perspective by comparing the urban structures of two very different cities. Most of the factors of location, which have been described previously, have been analyzed in the case of a single metropolitan area in a monocentric urban region. By measuring logistics sprawl in different metropolitan areas located in two different urban regions, one monocentric and one polycentric, we want to test the robustness of those factors and emphasize the importance of the structure of the urban region.

## 3 Logistics sprawl in the Paris and Randstad metropolitan areas

### 3.1 Method and data

The urban region of Paris (the Ile-de-France region), with 12 million inhabitants on 12,000 km$^2$, consists of nearly 1,300 municipalities. Ile-de-France is the largest consumer market in France, which demands an efficient logistics organization. The region, which represents 25% of the country's population, and 30% of its GDP, contains approximately 20% of France's total warehousing space. The transportation and logistics sectors account for almost 10% of employment in the region (about 400,000 jobs). Between 2000 and 2012, the Paris region experienced a 33% increase in the number of its warehousing facilities.

The Randstad region in the Netherlands, with 7.1 million inhabitants, includes 183 municipalities over 8,300 km$^2$. It is not an administrative entity, but the product of collective construction, gradually becoming included in the Dutch planning process. The term, literally meaning "border city", was coined in 1930 by a pilot who had noticed the peculiar urban form that extended from Rotterdam to Utrecht, surrounding a vast natural area ("Groene Hart" or Green Heart) (Kühn 2003). This term was adopted by public authorities in planning documents in the 1950s and has been steadily gaining currency since (Burke 1966). In 1966, Peter Hall (2008) described the Randstad. His notion of "metropolis" is still being debated today, for example in the most recent national planning document "Randstad Strategic Agenda 2040" (van der Burg, Vink 2008). The region is made up of four provinces (Noord Holland, Zuid Holland, Flevoland and Utrecht), which contain some of the largest cities in the Netherlands (Amsterdam, Rotterdam, The Hague and Utrecht). The Randstad represents 45% of the population of the Netherlands on 25% of its land and is the main gateway as well as goods consumption area in the Netherlands, in which respect it is comparable with metropolitan Paris. The Randstad region is a polycentric urban region clearly identified as a cultural, social, or political entity, which makes it an interesting case study.

This study aims to present comparable data for the two metropolitan areas. We used two databases: 'Local Knowledge of the Productive System' (CLAP) provided by INSEE (National Statistics Institute) for the French data and the Lisa database for the Dutch data. These two databases have the advantage that both use the NACE (Statistical Classification of Economic Activities in the European Community), so we can use the same categories for our comparison. We chose to use Category 52.1 "Storage". This category applies to activities that require a logistics building, namely a warehouse. In this category, the floor size of warehouses is not specified. According to DRIEA (2009), about 20% of the warehouses in the Paris region are less than 5,000m$^2$. Our databases also lack precision because they do not include all logistics buildings of the "warehouse" type. This is because the NACE classification only considers the principal purpose of a building, so some warehouses that serve the parcel industry or the distribution sector may not be recognized. The classification used by NACE and by extension the CLAP and Lisa databases have many shortcomings, which make it difficult to obtain an accurate estimate of the number of establishments and their location. Because of these limitations, the final number of logistics facilities presented in this study is only an estimate of the total.

We used the aggregated number of warehouses in municipalities for the years 2004 and 2012 for Ile-de-France and for the years 2007 and 2013 for the Randstad. Although the dates are not the same, as we did not have access to the exact same year, they are quite close from each other. Both allow us to understand how the location of these facilities has changed since the mid-2000s. Another comparability problem for these data is the great difference in the size of the municipalities in the two countries. In Ile-de-France the average size of municipalities is 10 km$^2$ with a population density in each municipality of 9,000 inhabitants per km$^2$ while in the Netherlands it is 86 km$^2$ with a density of about 1,000 inhabitants per km$^2$. To overcome this problem, we chose to use statistics for 'cantons' (an electoral jurisdiction) in Ile-de-France. The most rural municipalities have thus been grouped together, while those in the densest cities have remained separate. This particular division of the territory allows us to have a similar population in each division and just 286 statistical entities in Ile-de-France, which makes it possible to make a comparison between the two areas. This limitation does not fully allow us to compare the population densities and integration of warehouses in the metropolitan structure in absolute terms. We will make relative comparisons in view of the different situation in the two countries.

We have used a basic but robust spatial analysis indicator known as the centrographic method. This allows us to measure the changes in the distribution of a statistical population (in our case, warehouses) in space and over time, through the use of several indicators. We have calculated the mean distance of the warehouses in the two regions and in each province of the Randstad (we used the provincial unit for ease of data access and processing). Each Randstad province contains a rather well defined monocentric urban structure (with the exception of Flevoland, with no major city). To measure sprawl, we used the change in the average distance of terminals to their center of gravity. We used the calculation method that is included in the ArcGIS software (Mitchell 2005). The data on warehouses is aggregated for each province of the Randstad region and for each canton for the metro area of Paris. We weighted each province and canton by the number of warehouses.

### 3.2  Measuring logistics sprawl in the Paris and Randstad regions

The first observation of interest is that at macro-level scale, the two regions have experienced a different situation regarding logistics sprawl, with a deconcentration of logistics facilities in the Paris region (+5 km) and a contraction in the Randstad region. In the same time we observed an increasing number of warehouses in the Paris region (+33%) and stagnation in the Randstad (-1%). Not only are spatial dynamics different in the two but also the state of the logistics real estate market.

The Paris metropolitan area experienced a considerable degree of warehouse deconcentration between 2004 and 2012, since the average distance of the warehouses from their center of gravity increased by 4.1 km between these two years. This finding backs up the conclusions reached by an analysis of the parcel industry from the 1970s to 2010 (Dablanc, Rakotonarivo 2010) and of all warehouses during the last fifteen years (Heitz, Dablanc 2015). Our new analysis shows that logistics sprawl has continued in the Paris region (Ile-de-France) and the Paris metropolitan area ('Grand Paris') between 2010 and 2012.

The second observation is the heterogeneous nature of logistics spatial dynamics in the different provinces of the Randstad. The provinces of Noord Holland and Zuid Holland underwent contraction around the center of gravity. Indeed, the average distance from the center of gravity has fallen by -2 km in the province of Noord Holland and by -1 km in that of Zuid Holland. Although this is a relatively small decrease, it shows the existence of a dynamic in both provinces during the last years. Noord Holland is the province of the City of Amsterdam, which has attracted many service activities. The province of Zuid Holland is the largest of the Randstad and contains the conurbation between Rotterdam and The Hague, with several centers.

The observed geographic patterns of change may be a result of both centripetal forces

Table 1: Spatial indicators

|  | Regions | | Metro areas | | | | |
|---|---|---|---|---|---|---|---|
|  | Paris Region (Ile-de-France) | Randstad | Metro area of Paris ('Grand Paris') | Noord Holland (Amsterdam) | Zuid Holland (Rotterdam) | Flevoland | Utrecht |
| Time period | 2004-2012 | 2007-2013 | 2004-2012 | 2007-2013 | 2007-2013 | 2007-2013 | 2007-2013 |
| Area (km$^2$) | 12,012 | 8,357 | 657 | 2670 | 2818 | 1419 | 1450 |
| Population (million) | 11.9 | 8.5 | 4.5 | 2.7 | 3.6 | 0.4 | 1.2 |
| Number of warehouses (most recent year) | 955 | 583 | 441 | 278 | 185 | 59 | 61 |
| Number of warehouses (most ancient year) | 713 | 589 | 388 | 318 | 168 | 60 | 43 |
| Change in number of warehouses (%) | +34 | -1 | +14 | -12 | +10 | -2 | +42 |
| Logistics sprawl indicator (km) | 5 | — | 4.1 | -2 | -1 | 3.3 | 0.5 |

and centrifugal ones at the Randstad level. Logistics sprawl at the Randstad regional level may translate into concentration or deconcentration at the local scale (for each metropolitan area). The Randstad region experienced a dispersion of logistics activities in the 1970s when they moved from clusters to peripheral regions within the Netherlands (Davydenko et al. 2013). Nevertheless, our analysis measures these patterns in more detail and, also seems to suggest a coordinated move of centers of gravity towards the "Groene Hart", i.e. sprawl into the heart of the ring-shaped Randstad area, along the direction of the main highways connecting the cities. The provinces of Zuid Holland and Noord Holland have a different situation regarding the evolution of the number of warehouses. In the province of Zuid Holland the number of warehouses has increased by 10% while the number of warehouses has fallen in the province of Noord Holland by 12%. The absence of logistics growth and of logistics sprawl in Noord Holland means that Amsterdam metropolitan area as a logistics cluster is shrinking. Meanwhile, logistics facilities are growing inside the dense part of the Rotterdam metro area.

The deconcentration of warehouses is a confirmed pattern in the provinces of Utrecht and Flevoland. The province of Utrecht is small and polarized by the city of Utrecht. Flevoland province is slightly different from the others: it does not include major cities such as Amsterdam and Rotterdam nor major transport infrastructures, and in historical terms it is a recent creation. It cannot therefore be considered as an urban center in the same way as the others, but it is the subject of many proactive development policies, particularly for its new town of Almere. The deconcentration of warehouses is taking place in the provinces of Flevoland (+3.3 km) and Utrecht (+0.5 km), although the intensity of the process is not the same, being relatively low in the province of Utrecht compared with Flevoland. We can hypothesize that the significant deconcentration taking place in the Flevoland province is linked to the recent nature of its development.

By using the centrographic method, we have been able to determine whether warehouses have expanded or contracted around the urban centers. While it allowed us to observe the expansion of logistics activities in metropolitan areas, it did not allow us to say whether there was a pattern of logistics suburbanization, as we defined it above. We must supplement this discussion with an analysis of the integration of warehouses in relation to the density of metropolitan areas.

### 3.3  Measuring logistics suburbanization

To measure logistics suburbanization, we have established a profile for each municipality for the Randstad and each statistical canton for Ile-de-France, according to two criteria: firstly population density, and secondly the number of warehouses, which to some extent reflects logistics intensity. We have used the same data as before: the number of establishments classified as "warehouses" in the CLAP data for Paris and the Lisa data for the Randstad. These municipal (or cantonal) profiles were prepared using quartile-based discretization for each of the studied variables (population density and number of logistics facilities). This gave sixteen profiles. For ease of understanding we have grouped these profiles together to form four major types (see Table 2 and Figure 1).

Once the profile of each municipality has been assigned to one of the four possible types, we have calculated which profiles are overrepresented in order to identify the dominant patterns in each metropolitan area and obtain a specific picture of logistics sprawl (Figure 1). The cantons corresponding to the profile "A" have a population density of 11,687.5 inhabitants/km$^2$ in the Paris region compared with 594 inhabitants/km$^2$ in the Randstad. The profiles at each date and the way they have changed show the pattern of logistics sprawl that has taken place in the metropolitan areas.

Figure 1 shows how logistics activities are integrated within the metropolitan areas of each region and how they have changed over time.

In the case of Paris, the overrepresented profiles were types A and D in 2004, while in 2012 it was types B and C. In recent years, more warehouses have been set up in suburban towns than in municipalities with a higher population density. We do observe logistics suburbanization in the Paris region. This observation concurs with the work of Raimbault, Bahoken (2014) on logistics suburbanization. Logistics activities are declining in the densest areas and tending to favor less dense areas in the outer suburbs or the first

Table 2: Typology of municipality/canton profiles

| Profile | Type | Description |
| --- | --- | --- |
| A | Logistics in dense areas | High population density<br>High number of logistics establishments |
| B | Logistics in suburbs | Low population density<br>High number of logistics establishments |
| C | Residential zones | High population density<br>Low number of logistics establishments |
| D | Rural zones | Low population density<br>Low number of logistics establishments |

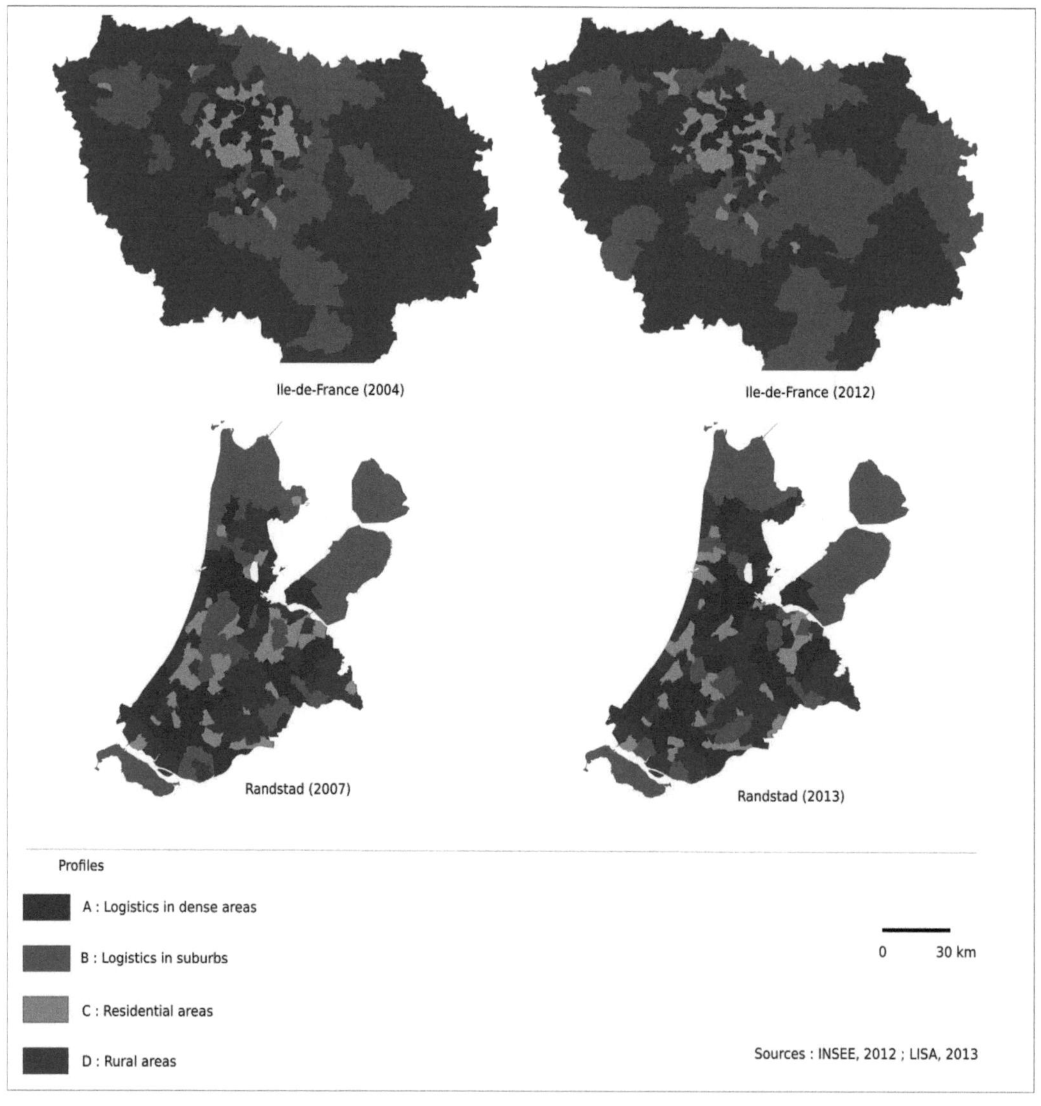


Figure 1: Comparison between local profiles in the Paris and Randstad regions

suburban ring. Logistics sprawl in metropolitan Paris has the effect of strengthening and densifying peripheral areas. The change in the location of the warehouses results not only in the expansion of the metropolitan area but also the increasing presence of logistics in the outskirts, in less densely populated areas.

In the Randstad region, municipalities with types A and D profiles dominate, both in 2007 and 2013. This means that logistics activities continue to locate in the dense areas of the region. Logistics suburbanization is much weaker than in Paris.

What is particularly striking in the analysis of the integration of warehouses in the metropolitan structure of Paris is the change in the location pattern between 2004 and 2012. Over this short period, there was a profound change. Logistics activities today seem to locate mainly in the suburbs where their numbers are growing. This analysis reveals that the warehouse location pattern goes beyond the deconcentration of logistics activities: logistics suburbanization is the dominant model. In contrast, in spite of the deconcentration of warehouses in certain urban conurbations, the Randstad exhibits weak logistics sprawl as well as logistics suburbanization, focused towards the inside of the ring-shaped region. Its dense areas have remained the prime location for logistics activities.

In recent years, modifications in the location of warehouses have generated spatial and morphological changes in cities (Frémont 2015). Overall, logistics facilities in the Paris and Randstad regions have become more dispersed. At the metropolitan scale, the Rotterdam and Amsterdam metro areas have an atypical profile and their warehouses have concentrated. They have not experienced logistics decentralization. In metropolitan Paris, the number of logistics sites has increased in peripheral areas to the detriment of the central areas, which means that logistics urbanization takes the form of logistics suburbanization. In summary, the case of the Randstad reveals the existence of a different form of logistics urbanization, logistics intensification, which we will discuss in the next section.

In section 2 we have identified different factors of relocation of logistics facilities mentioned in the literature. To explain the different forms of logistics locational patterns between the Paris and Randstad regions, we look at some of these factors in more detail.

## 4 Analysis of drivers explaining locational patterns: logistics suburbanization vs. logistics intensification

### 4.1 *The provision of airports and large logistics clusters*

Logistics facilities often tend to locate within logistics clusters in the fringes of metropolitan areas close to major airports and seaports or even highway networks (Hesse 2002, Woudsma et al. 2008, Cidell 2011, Allen et al. 2012). A freight transport system mainly performed by trucks contributes to logistics sprawl. In the Paris region, 90% of goods (in tonnes) are carried by road. Road accessibility is one of the most important factors of relocation of logistics facilities in the suburbs. Distance to the center is compensated by accessibility. A first movement of decentralization of transport infrastructure such as freight rail facilities in the 1960s and 1970s took away some logistics facilities from city centers to peripheral areas (Beyer 1999). In Paris, the development of logistics activities in peripheral areas is in part explained by the location of major transport nodes in these areas: Roissy and Orly airports, the river ports of Gennevilliers and Bonneuil, for example. These nodes still retain large clusters of warehouses (Heitz, Dablanc 2015). It so happens that the three major clusters in the innermost suburbs to the north (Gennevilliers), northeast (Roissy, Mitry-Mory) and south (Orly and Bonneuil) are also the main gateways for national and regional freight. These clusters are located in the peripheral areas. In the case of Paris, the location of nodal transportation infrastructure is an important factor of relocation of logistics facilities.

The Randstad region contains the port of Rotterdam, which is the largest (in terms of freight traffic) maritime port in Europe, and the Amsterdam Schiphol airport which is the fourth largest in Europe. The port of Rotterdam and its entire region are integrated in port regionalization dynamics, which means that logistics activities spread out into the region. Many activities are functionally linked to the port, and spread over a region that stretches from Dordrecht to Venlo through Tilburg (Priemus, Visser 1995) crossing the boundaries of municipalities and provinces (van der Burg, Vink 2008). However, it seems that this dynamic has been reversed in the provinces of Noord Holland and Zuid Holland in the last fifteen years. This observation allows us to appreciate how quickly the location of warehouses can change. The port of Rotterdam and Schiphol airport are the two most important logistics clusters in the Randstad (OECD 2007) and therefore naturally have a high concentration of warehouses and other logistics activities. In Zuid Holland in recent decades the port of Rotterdam has sought to limit its spatial expansion. The port of Rotterdam has decided to promote logistics development in the vicinity of port infrastructure. The Havenplan 2010 Port Development Plan emphasized the importance of limiting the space taken up by port development with the construction of the Second Maasvlakte, a polder in the North Sea near Rotterdam, and the relocation of activities (Priemus, Visser 1995). The decision to build this landfill was taken in 2004 and the facility was opened in 2013, thereby halting the expansion of the port towards the city and allowing re-urbanization of industrial areas. In anticipation of increased activity in the port, logistics activities have been redistributed around the port in recent years. The intensification of logistics reflects the existence of a new clustering of logistics activities highlighted by van den Heuvel et al. (2013).

Among the main factors for the development of logistics activities in the suburbs is a need for accessibility. Therefore, a possible explanation of logistics intensification is the severe congestion facing the area on the roads that connect the major urban centers. "Road congestion in the Netherlands is one of the most urgent problems facing the Port of Rotterdam, as it increases and decreases delivery time reliability for logistics companies that have chosen to use Rotterdam" (OECD 2007). Congestion can be a factor that limits logistics sprawl if its cost becomes excessive.

### 4.2　The role of public policies on logistics locational patterns

Dablanc, Raimbault (2015) argue that, despite attempts to achieve regional organization, the institutional fragmentation of metropolitan areas in France and the US lets "the laws of a dynamic land market and the most local level of government decide the location of logistics facilities" (p.301). A new logistics real estate in the outskirts of metropolitan areas reinforces the suburbanization of logistics, closely related to a lack of planning at the metropolitan level. With a long tradition of planning to address urban sprawl (Bogaerts et al. 2007), Dutch planners have de facto limited the sprawl of economic functions at a metropolitan scale. Suburban development took place in "quite a deconcentrated manner along the highways, at infrastructure nodes and on designated sites" (Bogaerts et al. 2007), but always limited by the "Groene Hart". Logistics deconcentration, as a result, appears to be quite limited in comparison with Paris. At the metropolitan scale, centripetal forces remain important, encouraged by policies focused on transport infrastructures, and logistics activities decentralize mostly along the highways. The polycentric region of the Randstad, overall, favors logistics concentration.

It is our hypothesis that this concentration is reinforced by public policies at the local and metropolitan levels. Public policies in the Netherlands have traditionally mainly focused on (1) developing the position of the Randstad as a hub for distributing goods across Europe; and (2) protecting the region's environment and contributing to the efforts against climate change. In the vision entitled "Randstad Holland in 2040" (Ministerie van Volkshuisvesting, Ruimtelijke Ordening en Milieu 2008), the government set out its plan to make the Randstad into a "sustainable, competitive top European region", considering the metropolitan region as a whole, which must become more homogeneous. With the plan "Randstad Holland in 2040", public authorities want to group together the "city regions" which are unequally developed, to form a coherent morphological and functional entity. This may help promote logistics intensification in the region. In Paris likewise, public policies have recently considered logistics sprawl. The recent regional master plan (SDRIF 2013) recommends the preservation of logistics activities in dense areas of the region and the promotion of tools to accommodate new logistics activities in the central areas. The new Paris municipal zoning code (Ville de Paris 2016) identifies more than 80 central city locations reserved for future logistics activities.

The Netherlands has a long tradition of urban planning. From the 1950s to the 2000s, a specific idea of the Randstad has predominated in the planning of the region influencing the location of economic activities. In 1958, the Randstad was defined as a group of "city regions" arranged in a horseshoe shape and separated by natural buffers including a large central green area. Urbanization is concentrated in the main urban centers and along the main roads connecting them (Rijksdienst voor het Nationale Plan 1958). The history of planning in the Randstad consists of successive policies promoting the development of compact cities and limiting urban sprawl by controlling the development of activities and the population on the region. In 1993, the Dutch Parliament adopted the "Supplement to the Fourth Policy on Territorial Planning", or VINEX. By favoring a compact city model, the Parliament tried to regulate mobility, increase the capacity of urban infrastructure, and protect natural spaces, for example with the ABC location policy ("ABC-locatiebeleid") (Bogaerts et al. 2007), which intended to plan the location of trip generators such as businesses, services, and industry. The location of economic activities was reorganized on the basis of the number of jobs in order to maximize the use of public transport. Activities involving fewer jobs and greater dependency on motorway access, such as warehouses, were encouraged to move to the outskirts, reserving the most densely populated areas for office type activities. The ABC location policy was then updated by policies that encourage the concentration of activities, including activities with lower density of jobs such as logistics. If the efficiency of these policies has been discussed, the Dutch planning system leaves considerable room for local spatial policy initiative and power.

Therefore, we could make the hypothesis that the concentration of warehouses around the main urban centers is a direct consequence of the desire of the Dutch government to encourage the concentration of urbanization. At the local level, the development of each urban center is a way of achieving a balance in the region. The project to develop the Randstad as an institution also aims to make a coherent area, based on a functionalist approach to space and on a division of functions between the economic centers in order to make them more specialized, intensify their activities, and improve their connectedness (van der Burg, Vink 2008). Rotterdam was identified as the main hub for the development of logistics and freight transport, Utrecht as a university center, The Hague as a political cluster that focuses on international law, and Amsterdam as the capital city, retaining the role of a multifunctional center. This distribution of functions is based on a particular concentration of economic activity around the various centers, especially around each of the major transport hubs, for example the ports of Rotterdam and Amsterdam or Schiphol airport.

We argue that logistics intensification may be partly due to the Randstad urban region's structure (polycentrism) and partly due to the public policies of concentration and preservation of green spaces. Parallel to these, 'relative densities' between urban centers and suburban areas may also be identified as an explanatory variable: a hypothesis can be that when the difference in density levels within a metro area is relatively minor, the availability of land or the differences in rental prices are not strong incentives to site a warehouse out of an urban center. A comparative analysis of densities and warehouses' rental prices in our two urban regions is still required to conclude on that matter.

While logistics sprawl has occurred in some provinces in the Randstad region, warehouse development in peripheral areas has not taken place at the expense of dense areas across the region. The dynamic expansion that we have described corresponds to logistics facilities' decentralization but it has not led to logistics facilities in peripheral areas dominating those in dense urban centers. In Amsterdam and Rotterdam metro areas logistics activities relocated around urban centers. This situation continued to apply between 2007 and 2013. Despite the presence of a strong sprawl dynamic affecting warehouses in the provinces of Flevoland (The Hague) and Utrecht, logistics is overall well integrated within dense areas. We can assume that The Hague and Utrecht have been experiencing logistics development later than Amsterdam and Rotterdam, and that logistics sprawl there is related to suburban sprawl. Overall, the Randstad example shows that dense areas can remain attractive for logistics activities. Analysis of the spatial dynamics in the Randstad reveals above all the existence of a form of urban logistics in which logistics activities remain a permanent feature of dense areas and in which areas of medium density undergo development. This can be called "logistics intensification".

Two forms, at least, of logistics urbanization coexist in metropolitan areas in Europe: logistics suburbanization and logistics intensification. In the case of the Paris region, logistics sprawl leads to logistics suburbanization, meanwhile the Randstad region experienced logistics contraction and densification. Public policies can explain some of the differences between logistics suburbanization and logistics intensification.

## 5   Conclusion

It has been observed in the literature that in many of the world's cities the development of logistics facilities has taken place in the outskirts as part of a process of logistics sprawl. However, it is noteworthy that most of these analyses were made in the case of monocentric urban regions, which contain one central urban area, highly developed suburbs, and less developed exurban areas. By analyzing changes in the location of warehouses in the polycentric Randstad region between 2007 and 2013, we highlighted the existence of another "model". Logistics intensification has occurred in the main urban areas (Rotterdam and Amsterdam) of the Randstad, with different distribution densities and center/suburb relationships. We have shown that each metro area of the Randstad has its own dynamic in terms of logistics. In the Randstad, logistics activities and warehouses tend to concentrate in (close to) metro areas, and we may relate that to its polycentric structure as well as (under links that remain to be specifically analyzed) its situation as a European freight hub and gateway. The specific tradition of land use control in the Randstad may also explain the intensification of logistics development in or close to the urban areas.

The different forms of logistic urbanization reveal a variable level of warehouse integration in metropolitan structures. Logistics activities are not condemned to "flee" into the suburbs. Under certain conditions, these activities can stay in the denser parts of a conurbation. We therefore formulate as a general conclusion that the diversity in the forms taken by logistics development is not simply due to the logistics and freight transport system, but also depends on the intrinsic characteristics of the regional spatial structure as well as local planning and land use policies.

This research cannot provide a final conclusion on the different types of logistics spatial developments according to the monocentric or polycentric nature of an urban region. In our two cases, the Paris region and the Randstad region, the intensification of logistics reflects a polycentric urban region while logistics suburbanization appears to be a symptom of a monocentric metropolitan area, but other factors, as we have shown, have played a role. This work is a starting point. What remains to be done, and could be relevant for a subsequent research about polycentric urban regions, is to look at freight and logistics interdependencies (freight flows to and from warehouses, main freight generators and consumption areas) between the four different provinces of the Randstad.

## Acknowledgement

This article presents results of a research carried out for the MetroFreight Center of Excellence on urban freight. MetroFreight is financed by the Volvo Research and Educational Foundations (VREF). For this research, the author benefited from an academic exchange with TU Delft (September 2014).

## References

Aljohania K, Thompson R (2016) Impacts of logistics sprawl on the urban environment and logistics: Taxonomy and review of literature. *Journal of Transport Geography* 57: 255–263. CrossRef.

Allain R (2004) Morphologie urbaine, géographie, aménagement et architecture de la ville. Armand Colin, Collection U, Paris

Allen J, Browne M, Cherrett T (2012) Investigating relationships between roadfreight-transport, facility location, logistics management and urban form. *Journal of Transport Geography* 24: 45–57. CrossRef.

Berroir S, Mathian H, Saint-Julien T, Sanders M (2008) La mobilité dans la construction du polycentrisme métropolitain. In: Thiérault M, Des Rosiers F (eds), *Information Géographique et dynamiques Urbaines 1*. Hermes-Lavoisier, collection, IGAT, 31–57

Beyer A (1999) Morphologies et dynamiques territoriales des services de messagerie. doctoral thesis, Université Paris XII

Bogaerts A, Dieleman F, Dijst M, Geertman S (2007) Economic deconcentration in a rational planning system: The Dutch case. In: Razin E, Dijst M, Vázquez C (eds), *Employment Deconcentration in European Metropolitan Areas: Market Forces versus Planning Regulations*. Springer, Dordrecht. CrossRef.

Bowen J (2008) Moving places: The geography of warehousing in the US. *Journal of Transport Geography* 16[6]: 379–87. CrossRef.

Burke G (1966) *Green Heart Metropolis: Planning the Western Netherlands*. Macmillan, Toronto

Champion A (2001) A changing demographic regime and evolving polycentric urban regions: Consequences for the size, composition and distribution of city populations. *Urban Studies* 38[4]: 657–677. CrossRef.

Cidell J (2010) Concentration and decentralization: The new geography of freight distribution in US metropolitan areas. *Journal of Transport Geography* 18[3]: 363–71. CrossRef.

Cidell J (2011) Distribution centers among rooftops: the global logistics network meets the suburban spatial imaginary. *International Journal of Urban and Regional Research* 35[4]: 832–851. CrossRef.

Dablanc L, Raimbault N (2015) Penser autrement la métropole logistique: questions d'aménagement et d'urbanisme. In: Dablanc L, Frémont A (eds), *La métropole logistique, Le transport de marchandises et le territoire des grandes villes*. Armand Colin, Paris

Dablanc L, Rakotonarivo D (2010) The impacts of logistic sprawl: How does the location of parcel transport terminals affect the energy efficiency of goods' movements in Paris and what can we do about it? *Procedia. Social and Behavioral Sciences* 2[3]: 6087–6096. CrossRef.

Dablanc L, Ross C (2012) Atlanta: A mega logistics center in the Piedmont Atlantic Megaregion (PAM). *Journal of Transport Geography* 24: 432–442. CrossRef.

Davoudi S (2003) Polycentricity in European spatial planning: from an analytical tool to a normative agenda. *European Planning Studies* 6[4]: 365–377. CrossRef.

Davydenko I, Tavasszy L, Quak H (2013) A quantitative model for exploration of logistics sprawl of the future. Metrans conference http://www.metrans.org/sites/default/files/-Metrans_Davydenko_Tavasszy_Quak.pdf

DRIEA (2009) Étude sur l'estimation et la caractérisation du parc d'entrepôts en Ile-de-France. http://www.driea.ile-de-france.developpement-durable.gouv.fr/IMG/pdf/-Estimation_parcentrepots_GRECAM_cle651884.pdf (last accessed Feb 17, 2017)

Frémont A (2015) Introduction. In: Dablanc L, Frémont A (eds), *La métropole logistique. Le transport de marchandises et le territoire des grandes villes*. Armand Colin, Paris, 9–18

Hall P (2008) How polycentric are mega-city regions? Nova terra, January, 24-29

Hall P, Hesse M (2013) Cities, flows and scale. policy responses to the dynamics of integration and disintegration. In: Hall P, Hesse M (eds), *Cities, Regions and Flows*. Routledge, London, 247–259

Heitz A, Dablanc L (2015) Logistics spatial patterns in Paris: The rise of the Paris basin as a logistics megaregion. *Transportation Research Record: Journal of the Transportation Research Board* 2477: 76–84

Hesse M (2002) Location matters. ACCESS magazine. University of California Transportation Center, 21, 22-26

Hesse M (2004) Land for logistics: locational dynamics, real estate markets and political-regulation of regional distribution complexes. *Tijdschrift voor economische en sociale geografie* 95[2]: 162–173. CrossRef.

Kühn M (2003) Greenbelt and green heart: separating and integrating landscapes in European city regions. *Landscape and urban planning* 64: 19–27. CrossRef.

Lasserre F (2004) Logistics and the internet: transportation and location issues are crucial in the logistics chain. *Journal of Transport Geography* 12[1]: 73–84. CrossRef.

Le Nechet F, Aguiléra A (2012) Forme urbaine et mobilité domicile-travail dans 13 aires urbaines françaises: une analyse multiéchelle. *Recherche Transports et Sécurité* 28[3-4]: 259–270

Merenne-Schoumaker B (2008) La localisation des grandes zones de logistique. *Bulletin de la Société géographique de Liège* 49: 31–40

Ministerie van Volkshuisvesting, Ruimtelijke Ordening en Milieu (2008) Randstad Holland in 2040, environment and spatial planning. Strategic document

Mitchell A (2005) Manuel ESRI d'analyse SIG. 2. Paris, ESRI Press

Nicot B (1996) Une mesure de l'étalement urbain en France, 1982-1990. *Revue d'Economie Régionale et Urbaine* 1: 71–98

OECD (2007) Randstad Holland, Netherlands. OECD Territorial Reviews

Priemus H, Visser J (1995) Infrastructure policy in the Randstad Holland: struggle between accessibility and sustainability. *Political Geography* 14[4]: 363–377. CrossRef.

Raimbault N (2015) Grande distribution: entre performance logistique et contrainte foncière. In: Dablanc L, Frémont A (eds), *La métropole logistique, Le transport de marchandises et le territoire des grandes villes*. Armand Colin, 161–178

Raimbault N, Bahoken F (2014) Quelles places pour les activités logistiques dans la métropole parisienne? *Territoire en Mouvement* 23-24: 53–74. CrossRef.

Rijksdienst voor het Nationale Plan (1958) Netherlands. werkcommissie westen des lands. Staatsdrukkerij en uitgeverijbedrijf

SDRIF – Schéma directeur de la région Île-de-France (2013) Schéma directeur de la région Île-de-France. https://www.iledefrance.fr/action-quotidienne/construire-ile-france-2030-0 (last accessed March 12, 2017)

van den Heuvel FP, de Langen PW, van Donselaar KH, Fransoo JC (2013) Spatial concentration and location dynamics in logistics: the case of a Dutch province. *Journal of Transport Geography* 28: 39–48. CrossRef.

van der Burg A, Vink B (2008) Randstad Holland 2040. 44th ISOCARP congress

Ville de Paris (2016) Plan Local d'Urbanisme de Paris. Document stratégique de planification

Woudsma C, Jakubicek P, Dablanc L (2015) Logistics sprawl in North America: methodological issues and a case study in Toronto. *Transportation Research Procedia* 12: 474–488. CrossRef.

Woudsma C, Jensen J, Kanaroglou P, Maoh H (2008) Logistics land use and the city: a spatial-temporal modeling approach. *Transportation Research Part E, Logistics and Transportation Review* 44[2]: 277–297. CrossRef.

REGION

The Journal of ERSA
Powered by WU

Volume 4, Number 1, 2017, 71–92
DOI: 10.18335/region.v4i1.172

journal homepage: region.ersa.org

# Potentials and limitations for the use of accessibility measures for national transport policy goals in freight transport and logistics: Evidence from Västra Götaland County, Sweden

Anders Larsson[1], Jerry Olsson[2]

[1] University of Gothenburg, Gothenburg, Sweden (email: anders.larsson@geography.gu.se)
[2] University of Gothenburg, Gothenburg, Sweden and University of Oxford, Oxford, UK
   (email: jerry.olsson@geography.gu.se)

Received: 28 October 2016/Accepted: 13 April 2017

**Abstract.** Swedish national transport policy treats freight transport as a major facilitator of economic development at all geographical levels. It is simultaneously noted that methods and data for business location and transportation are inadequate for following up transport policy objectives. This paper reports on a pilot study of the potential to develop accessibility measures to support and follow up policy objectives in the Swedish context. The accessibility concept and its practical application in concrete measures are discussed and problematized. Several practical examples from Västra Götaland County are used as illustrations. In terms of results, the study identifies several potentials and limitations of using accessibility measures to address freight transport issues. These measures' usefulness is driven mainly by the integration capability of transport and land use. This permits more complex questions and measures, supporting the integration between planning specializations. Limitations largely concern data availability and quality and the extent to which maps and measures can be communicated to non-experts. The concluding discussion highlights how the policy and governance context is central to understanding how best to utilize the potential strengths of the accessibility concept and related measures.

**Key words:** accessibility, freight transport, logistics facilities, transport policy

## 1 Introduction

Swedish national transport policy is intended to ensure that the transport system supports the country's economic development in a sustainable way, for example, by promoting the accessibility of logistics terminals, ports, and other transport infrastructure. It is simultaneously noted that methods and data for business location and transportation are inadequate for completely following up transport policy objectives in the field (Transport Analysis 2013a).

Shifts in the logistics sector have for quite some time illustrated a trend towards the consolidation of terminals, a trend expected to continue in the future (Hesse 2008, McKinnon 2009, Dablanc, Ross 2012, Sheffi 2012). This will lead to relatively fewer but larger units that may fundamentally change the accessibility of logistics services to businesses, especially those located outside major urban centres and transport corridors. It is therefore crucial that national and regional policymakers and planners better understand and follow up the shifting landscape of modern supply chains, as this underscores the importance of comprehensive efforts to coordinate land use, not only for logistics facilities but also other businesses that generate freight movements (Barysiene et al. 2015, David 2015, Sakai et al. 2015).

A key issue is the availability of data for both mapping current conditions and following change over time (Allen, Browne 2008). Freight flow data, for example, is only available at the crude geographical level of counties (Swedish Transport Administration 2013). One further explanation for the lack of comprehensive goals and targets is the heterogeneity of the freight transport market, in which each type of good has specific requirements and thus specific conditions and needs. This is sustained by the traditional institutional separation in which Swedish spatial planning is characterized by a two-level system based on the nation-state, at one level, and on local authorities with considerable autonomy, on the other. This system is not unique to Sweden (see David 2015 on land use planning in the United States). This has resulted in a division of spatial planning responsibilities, with strategic infrastructure and accessibility issues being handled at the national level, while local authorities are responsible for land-use planning, including business location. Although the last decade has witnessed growth in regional-level influence (Lindström 2007), there is still a substantial lack of coordination between actors at different geographical levels.

The Mobility Research Group at the Department of Economy and Society at the University of Gothenburg[1] has for several years worked on accessibility issues in personal transport, using a GIS-based model with high spatial resolution and connected to individual-level data (Elldér, Ernstson, Fransson, Larsson 2012). Several projects have been implemented, the most comprehensive one being implemented jointly with Västra Götaland Regional Planning Authority (Elldér, Gil Solá, Larsson 2012). This GIS-based model also has potential in the freight sector, as exemplified by recent research into city logistics and freight terminal utilization (Olsson, Woxenius 2012, 2014).

To pilot the methodological possibility of combining high spatial resolution with employment and industrial sector data, the Swedish government agency, Transport Analysis, has commissioned a project to test opportunities for better understanding regional patterns, accessibility potentials, and data requirements for accessibility analysis in freight transport (Olsson, Larsson 2016).

Within this context, the aim of this article is to *introduce and examine the potentials and limitations of accessibility analysis for monitoring policy goals in freight transport.* This scope can be specified in three research questions, as follows:

- What are the main strengths and weaknesses of the current accessibility approach relative to other similar concepts?

- How can accessibility measures be applied to freight transport problems?

- What are the most important strengths and limitations of accessibility analysis for monitoring transport policy goals?

The paper continues with a presentation and discussion of the accessibility concept and related measures, followed by a brief presentation of Swedish transport policy goals with a focus on freight transport. This presentation is then illustrated by examples of measures applied to Västra Götaland County. The results of the mapping and database analysis are brought together in the discussion section, which is followed by the presentation of conclusions.

---

[1] http://es.handels.gu.se/english/units/unit-for-human-geography/research/research-groups/mobility-research-group

## 2 From mobility to accessibility planning: concepts and measures

### 2.1 Introduction

Recent decades have witnessed increasing travel and increasing levels of car dependence in cities worldwide (Handy 2002, Banister 2005, 2008). Mobility has become taken for granted in people's everyday lives and in business strategy development. This has profound implications for the flows and relationships that build cities and regions. Simultaneously, cities are experiencing a range of mobility-related problems, such as congestion, lack of safety, noise, and air pollution, all imposing societal costs and affecting business productivity (Bertolini 2005, Melo et al. 2009).

These are obviously problems whose solutions call for an integrated, holistic approach. Traditional planning perspectives often separate the fields of infrastructure, land use, and business development, treating them as "silos" with little or no coordination. The concept of accessibility brings together transport/mobility and land use, offering a useful framework for more integrated planning strategies (Geurs, van Wee 2004, Ferreira et al. 2012). It also offers a potentially powerful guide that planning practitioners can employ to develop and test effective strategies for building sustainable cities and regions (Straatemeier 2008).

### 2.2 The accessibility concept

In the following, we refer to accessibility based on the following definition: "The extent to which the land use–transport system enables (groups of) individuals or goods to reach activities or destinations by means of a (combination of) transport mode(s)" (Geurs, Ritsema van Eck 2001, p. 19). This definition is based on four components:

- *Transportation*: the cost (e.g., time or monetary costs) of moving goods or people physically to a destination including all modes of transport.

- *Land use*: the location and geographical distribution of potential origin and destination points, such as population density, jobs, services, customers, and warehouses.

- *Time*: access to facilities and activities varies during the day depending on, for example, the operating hours of suppliers and customers.

- *Individual*: individual values, opportunities, needs, and constraints represent important conditions for the broad application of the accessibility concept.

In an early application to spatial planning, Hansen (1959) broadly defined accessibility as: "the potential of opportunities of interaction". This suggests two contrasting definitions of accessibility, one addressing how points in a network relate to each other (i.e., access to potential opportunities from one specific starting point), and another depicting how all points are related to all other points on a surface (i.e., general spatial potential). Ingram (1971) later referred to this distinction as being between relative and integral accessibility, respectively. Our point of departure is the relative approach, since we are interested in accessibility for specific purposes, travelling to/from specific activity points. Before exploring accessibility measures in greater detail, we would like to draw attention to several related concepts.

### 2.3 The relationship between accessibility, mobility, and proximity

Accessibility as defined above is related to the concept of mobility, since movement is a means to achieve accessibility. It includes all forms of physical movement using or not using vehicles as well as virtual movement using communication technology. Historically, we have witnessed progression towards increasing car-based mobility over gradually longer distances in order to facilitate accessibility. However, given current discussion of mobility and sustainability (Banister 2008), it is important to highlight the opposite strategy, namely, accessibility through proximity.

Figure 1 illustrates in a simplified way two principal approaches to achieving good accessibility, i.e., spatial proximity and overcoming distance. Achieving good accessibility

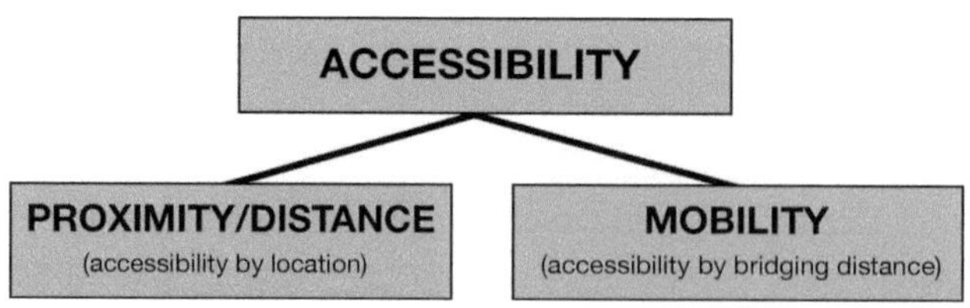


*Source*: Haugen 2012

Figure 1: The interrelationship between accessibility, mobility, and proximity

through proximity emphasizes the land-use component, with the importance of the location of points of production and consumption. Any improvement of accessibility then involves relocating either the origin or destination points, or both. The traditional policy solution to poor accessibility has been to concentrate on mobility by improving road infrastructure capacity, creating the potential to uphold reliable but potentially unsustainable transport systems over long distances.

This highlights a potential conflict between traditional transport-based planning and current land-use-based ideas of proximity- and non-car-based planning in cities (Newman, Kenworthy 2015). This debate has emanated from person-transport considerations but is as important for freight. We argue that this is one area where an accessibility approach provides a platform for the integration of transport and land use. It is important to note that normative measures are often needed in practical planning contexts (Páez et al. 2012), possibly leading to a situation in which opposing policy goals for transport and land use are present in the same accessibility measure.

These concepts and distinctions are fundamental, not only in an abstract theoretical sense but also in order to understand everyday planning problems. One example from personal transport is the so-called accessibility paradox (Haugen 2012, Haugen et al. 2012, Haugen, Vilhelmson 2013), in which measured reduced average travel times between residents and the nearest locations of important daily activities (e.g., schools and services) do not always correspond to shorter actual trip distances. Other factors and preferences (e.g., type of school and education) can be seen as more important than proximity. This illustrates that it is far from obvious that the relationship between accessibility, mobility, and distance is determined by a one-dimensional rational choice to minimize either distance or time. This is even more problematic in freight transport, in which decisions about route choice or terminal usage are made by several layers of actors and very rarely based on a shortest-distance logic (Melo et al. 2009).

Given this discussion, planning for improved accessibility in freight transport is complex. For example, it is important to critically examine for whom and where accessibility will be improved. Different firms at the same location might have very different accessibility needs and interests due to, for example, their types of goods, business sector, logistics management solution, customer density, and traffic congestion situation and to the effect of freight transport on local residents (Melo et al. 2009).

## 2.4 Overview of accessibility measures

To move from accessibility principles to implementation, we must look more closely at the most common accessibility measures. Geurs, van Wee (2004) identified four types of accessibility measures depending on the perspective or problem area considered: i) infrastructure-based, ii) activity-based (divided into location and space–time measures), iii) individual-based, and iv) utility-based measures. It is important to recall that, depending on the approach chosen, it is only possible to address a limited set of problems. Since this paper applies mainly location-based measures, we will emphasize these. However, a brief overview of other types of measures is given first.

An infrastructure approach to accessibility focuses on the properties of road, rail, bike, and walking networks, such as their connectivity and speed. These network properties provide a good indication of accessibility and mobility near where roads or railways and their nodes are located, but say less about accessibility over a wider hinterland. It is also difficult to measure, for example, the effect of increased road speed, as this is directly related to land-use factors such as population, jobs, and commuting (Geurs, Ritsema van Eck 2001).

Individual-based measures start at the individual level and consider the opportunities and limitations in performing activities at different locations during a given period, such as one day. The approach is largely based on a time-geographic approach (Hägerstrand 1970) in which the abilities of individuals or groups (e.g., households) to perform daily activities and projects are determined by individual and joint restrictions in time and space. Accessibility then becomes more complex than just being able to reach a certain point within a certain optimal distance or time. It also involves relationships with all other events and locations that need to be temporal-spatially coordinated during the day. When applied to freight transport and logistics, this approach might be used to better address limitations such as the opening hours of firms/suppliers/terminals and peak-hour congestion. This approach might be more applicable in a business context than in public land-use planning.

Based on economic utility theory, one can use businesses' valuations of the benefits of various alternative destinations as an accessibility measure. The assumed logic here is that decision makers make rational choices intended to maximize their own cost/benefit ratio. The advantage of this approach is that the measure has a strong theoretical coupling to economic theory. This is also its drawback, as considerable theoretical knowledge is required in order to understand such an abstract measure and how it can be implemented and communicated in practical planning (see La Paix, Geurs 2016).

*2.5 Location-based measures*

Location-based accessibility measures take into account both the transportation and the land-use components. In local or regional planning, this type of measure is considerably more relevant and is more widely applicable since it is directly linked to particular geographical areas and their demographic and socio-economic contexts. Such measures can range from straight-line distance or travel-time measures from one starting point to one or more destinations, to complex implementations of distance friction and the weighting of destination importance and competition.

The most straightforward measure is distance, either in absolute terms, such as the number of metres, or in relative terms, such as travel time. The aim is often to calculate either the number of potential customers or suppliers within a given catchment area or the closest destination(s) of interest. If we instead want to know how many warehouses (or other destinations) can be reached within a specific time interval, cumulative measures (i.e., contour or isochrone measures) are used. Breheny (1978) divided the accessibility of opportunities measure into three dimensions: starting points, destinations, and costs. By keeping one factor constant, it is possible to obtain a relatively easy-to-understand cumulative measure:

- *Keeping costs constant* measures the opportunities available within a certain cost in distance, time, or monetary terms; for example, the number of potential jobs reachable within a 30-minute trip.

- *Keeping target points constant* measures the cost of reaching a predetermined number of opportunities; for example, the average travel time across a region to reach 50% of the warehouses in that region.

- *Keeping the starting point constant* measures the potential opportunities based on variations in cost; for example, the number of warehouses within different travel-time intervals from a selected point.

These types of measures give results in the form of spatial distributions, allowing visualization in the form of influence fields or hinterlands. Figure 2 illustrates the spatial outcomes of these measures.

These metrics are useful in practical planning due to their relative simplicity and resulting communicability to a wider audience. This simplicity also presents problems,

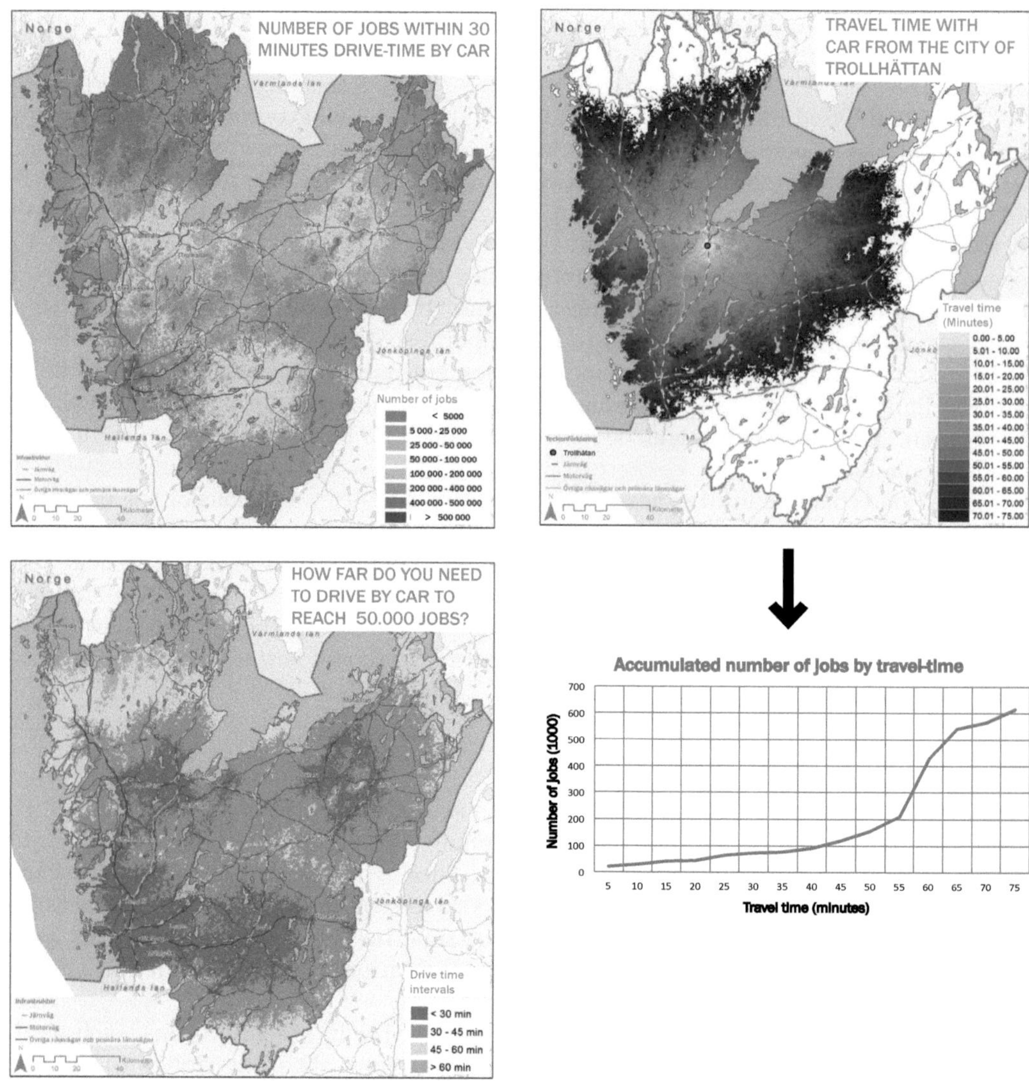


*Source*: sources: authors' calculations; road network, Swedish Transport Administration; other map data, Swedish Land Survey; socio-demographic data, Statistics Sweden

Figure 2: Illustrations of different accessibility measures using the same data: fixed cost (top left), constant target points (bottom left), constant starting point (top right), and potential jobs by travel time (bottom right)

however. An important limitation is that the used measures treat all target points as equally valuable, regardless of the travel time. It is important that the travel time and distance parameters be determined so as to reflect actual travel behaviour. For freight transport, this is a major limitation, since there is no direct equivalent to travel surveys in personal transport studies.

The value of distance can more realistically be calculated using functions to capture friction of distance, meaning that the farther away something is, the less its influence on the final result. The advantage of such metrics is that distance affects accessibility, enabling calculations based on empirical studies of actual travel behaviour. This yields more accurate and theoretically consistent results, which, however, may be difficult for outsiders to interpret. This approach also requires that function parameters be based on empirical travel surveys for them to be reliable for a specific region.

## 3 Swedish national transport policy goals for accessibility and freight transport

The overall Swedish national transport policy objective states that the transport system should contribute to economic development throughout the country. In terms of accessibility, this requires good access to logistics terminals, ports, and other road/rail transport infrastructure. At the same time, concerning the monitoring of transport policy objectives and methods, it has been found that access to data on business location and transportation is inadequate (Transport Analysis 2013b,c).

One basic prerequisite for the creation of measures that contribute to the more efficient use of transport system resources is reliable information on the location of freight transport-intensive operation facilities. Authorities with overall responsibility for the follow-up of policy goals, such as Transport Analysis (2013b,c), need quantitative information on the accessibility of important logistical destinations, such as ports and logistics centres, to various industries. There is currently a lack of appropriate indicators, as the disaggregated data are of insufficient quality.

A question, then, is whose perspective should be taken into account? As logistics and freight transport comprise disparate activities with varied requirements and conditions, different actors' logic, behaviour, and priorities frequently counteract each other. There is a risk of sub-optimization in which all actors streamline their transportation needs based on the conditions governing their specific operations. When these actors are highly autonomous, individual decisions are made without paying attention to the entire logistics chain (Ministry of Enterprise and Innovation 2011).

The Energy Commission's final report states that long-term investments in infrastructure and other planning need to target the creation of conditions for a more energy-efficient transport system (SOU 2008). From a national perspective, therefore, knowledge of business locations and of the accessibility of key nodes and hubs (including ports and airports) is central, as both long-term planning and investment are expected to concentrate on fewer transport nodes and designated freight transport corridors, as illustrated in the following quotation (Swedish Transport Administration 2013):

> In the national plan for the transport system, a strategic network for long-distance haulage is defined. The network includes a designated road/rail network, central intermodal terminals, ports, and airports. This network is considered to be of paramount importance for long-distance business freight transport. Therefore, Transport Administration actions should be concentrated on the strategic network. (Swedish Transport Administration 2013, p. 12)

This need to define a national core network follows partly because the distances within the country are great and partly because Sweden, as a major exporter, is very sensitive to the efficiency of increasingly spatially extended global transport networks. From a national perspective, industrial logistics costs are therefore central, from both the short-term competitive and long-term sustainability perspectives. However, the societal perspective has much broader significance, and the overall transport policy objective is to ensure economic efficiency for both business and citizens throughout the country. According to the Ministry of Enterprise and Innovation (2011), a priority is to increase the efficiency of freight transport and optimally use the existing infrastructure (increased infrastructure capacity cannot itself meet the entire expected increase in transport demand). From a societal perspective, therefore, logistics must be recognized as transportation activity wherein capacity, traffic environment (i.e., safety), accessibility, and energy consumption are taken into account for all users – including passengers. At the same time, these considerations need to be balanced by a good economic and business climate. Taken together, this calls for clear indicators for monitoring community investments in transportation and land use.

## 4   Accessibility measures and their application in freight transport: examples from Västra Götaland County

### 4.1   *Method, material, and limitations*

Accessibility measures and maps are calculated using purpose-built software initially developed for personal transport to combine advanced transport modelling of public transport with GIS functionality (Berglund 2001). This accessibility tool combines geo-referenced data with information about the transport system and travel options. It enables the computation of accessibility by both car and public transport of many potential supply points, such as amenities and workplaces.

For this study we have used only the capabilities related to movement along the road network. The computations were based on calculated travel times between $500 \times 500$-metre cells, allowing analysis beyond administrative divisions. For a more in-depth description of the tool functionality see Elldér, Ernstson, Fransson, Larsson (2012) and Larsson et al. (2014).

Each cell contained information on the number of logistics terminals and food-sector firms. Logistics terminals are defined as facilities for the reception, delivery, consolidation, distribution, and storage of freight in the transportation process. Food-sector firms comprise facilities covered by the Swedish industry classification code SNI 10, which covers the production of foodstuffs. This allows us to link driving times, land uses (or location patterns), and economic indicators on the production side of the logistics-sensitive food sector. We are aware that the distribution side of the food sector is also highly relevant in terms of logistics restructuring. However, a lack of detailed data on retailers and large-chain internal terminals limits the potential to include such information in this illustrative case. This issue is elaborated on in sections 5 and 6.

The data used in the analysis is drawn from several sources, as follows:

1. *Road network* data, including speed limits for calculating driving time, was supplied by the Swedish Transport Administration's National Road Database (NVDB) and captures the situation in September 2014.

2. Data on *logistics terminals*, including their exact locations, was updated by the authors based on a previous study by the government agency Traffic Analysis (WSP 2013). The services and activities that terminals offer can be captured only partially using statistical industry codes. These terminals may range from storage-only facilities to complete logistics centres incorporating a wide range of complementary services. Substantial time was spent manually qualifying the function of terminals.

3. Data on *multimodal rail–road terminals*, including location and capacity, was collected by the authors from company and public authority websites.

4. *Locations of food-sector firms* were extracted from the internal GILDA longitudinal database comprising official register data provided by Statistics Sweden. Individuals are linked to their workplaces, making it possible to identify the type of activity associated with all workplaces in the region.

The measures are calculated based on certain conditions and limitations due to incomplete data or limitations in the accessibility model. In this study, logistics terminals are limited to those open to all potential commercial customers. This definition is applied because it reflects the true geographical potential. We can find many additional facilities within company-internal logistics systems. However, these are not potential service points for outsiders even if located within reach according to accessibility calculations.

In some analyses we refer to large terminals, which are terminals with annual turnovers of SEK 100 million in 2014 (equivalent to USD 12.5 million). This demarcation is relevant in order to identify sites with enough capacity to supply customers with a variety of services.

As discussed elsewhere in this paper, cumulative accessibility measures are dependent on the setting of time limitations. In this case, 60 minutes of driving time is used as the threshold in several maps. This is based on the principle of centrality, whereby a terminal's hinterland comprises roughly 100 km (Rodrigue et al. 2013, p. 135). Exactly where the line is established on a commercial basis may vary between carriers.

A further distinction concerns potential customers. Different business sectors have very different requirements in terms of distances, terminal facilities, etc. In this study, we use the food industry as a proxy for logistics-intensive industries, representing the part of the economy that is dependent on flexible and frequent logistics chains for daily activities and that could potentially use the terminals. One important limitation of the calculations is that they include only terminals and food-sector production plants in Västra Götaland County. This limitation was made due to the very time-consuming process of identifying logistics terminals, elaborated on in section 5. Since both logistics providers and terminals compete, this limitation creates uncertainty as to the results in border regions. This is especially significant in the eastern part of the region, where a significant market is reachable by 30 minutes of driving.

We would also like to raise the issue of data categorization on maps. Visual perceptions, and hence the analytical values, of datasets are highly dependent on the selection of appropriate classes and categories (Evans 1977). For this paper, we selected classes according to the principle of simplicity in communication with non-expert groups; for example, travel times are divided into 15-minute intervals. It is important to note that other classification schemes might reveal a more extreme hierarchical pattern in the data (Jiang 2013), being more suitable for research questions comparing highly accessible areas with less accessible ones.

### 4.2 Accessibility measures based on driving time to nearest facility

The most straightforward geographical measure is driving time to the nearest terminal. Figure 3 shows the driving time to the nearest terminal, regardless of its size or function. The map clearly illustrates how virtually every part of the region has access to a terminal within 30 minutes.

The map in Figure 4 illustrates the calculated accessibility to large terminals expected to provide the range of services needed for customers not part of corporate logistics networks, such as those of Volvo or IKEA. Using only the major terminals as destinations, differences in driving time become more pronounced. Moreover, it is possible to discern several corridors along major highways with short travel times. This also illustrates the usefulness of disaggregated spatial units: the use of more aggregated spatial units, such as municipalities, could cause the corridor effects shown in the map to be overlooked.

Driving time is useful due to its uncomplicated form. However, to benefit from accessibility analysis, there is a need to add the land-use component. This is illustrated in Figure 5 by the number of companies in the food industry located within different driving-time intervals.

Adding the potential number of users in the logistics-sensitive food sector illustrates the concentration and co-location of warehouses and food-sector firms. Half of the firms are under 15 minutes from the nearest terminal and more than 80 % can be reached within 60 minutes. The difference between large terminals and all terminals widens with increased travel time, but does not exceed 10%.

The use of driving time as a measure has several advantages, mainly because the result in minutes is an absolute value and very easy to communicate. This indicator is directly related to everyday freight transport issues such as delivery time and precision. A further advantage is that it is relatively easy to calculate, needing only two datasets: road network and terminal locations. This makes it affordable to calculate and, from a data supply perspective, it is relatively easy to collect longitudinal datasets in order to monitor changes over time.

There are also limitations to using driving time as a measure. Its simplicity means that it addresses only a very specific question. For following up the Swedish national transport policy objectives, however, this measure is insufficient on its own. A further drawback is the use of travel time without weighting. For personal transport measures, it is common to add weights to the points of attraction and to use distance decay functions for the travelling. Here the logic is that the larger the city, the greater the attraction, and conversely, the farther away, the greater the resistance. This procedure is supposed to

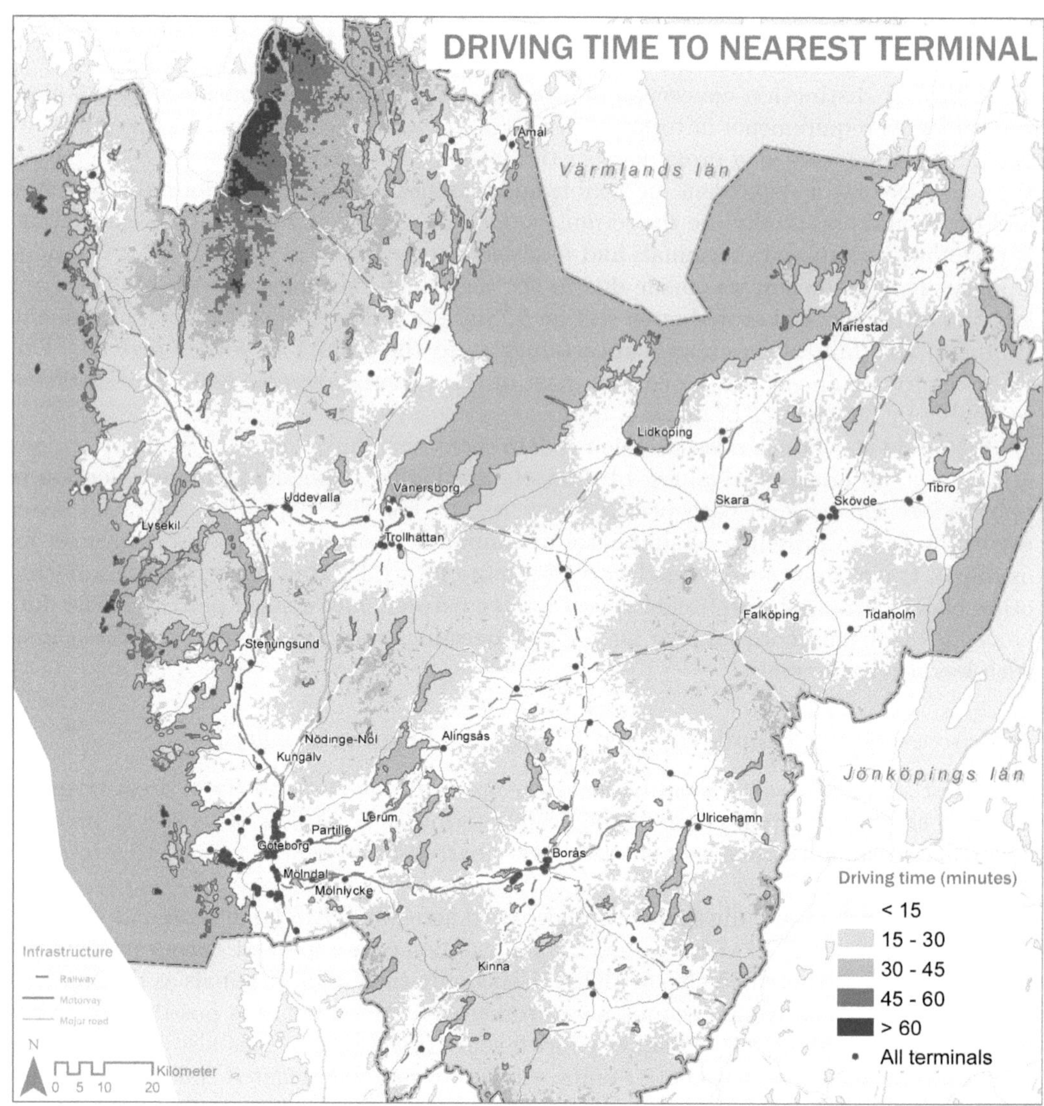



Figure 3: Accessibility in terms of driving time to the nearest terminal

make the analysis more realistic in relation to travel behaviour. The problem in freight transport calculations is lack of knowledge (mainly due to lack of primary data) of how goods actually move and of the criteria for the choices made. More knowledge of the "travel behaviour" of freight would be needed in order to determine whether, for example, the nearest terminal is actually a valid measure in real everyday situations.

### 4.3 Measures based on potential accessibility and catchment areas

While the measure used in Figures 3 and 4 illustrates accessibility from a transport buyers' perspective, the logic can be reversed and instead used to investigate the potential catchment areas of terminals, measured as the number of destinations reachable within a specific time. In this case, we have chosen 60 minutes of driving time.

The main advantage of this measure is that it connects infrastructure and space via potential, providing a clear basis for assessing what areas meet a certain objective or minimum requirement level. This measure is also relatively easy to communicate. Compared with the driving time indicator, catchment areas permit us to follow up municipalities' and regions' competitive potential in terms of how well they are situated in the terminal landscape.

However, one important limitation is the fact that the measure considers all destinations

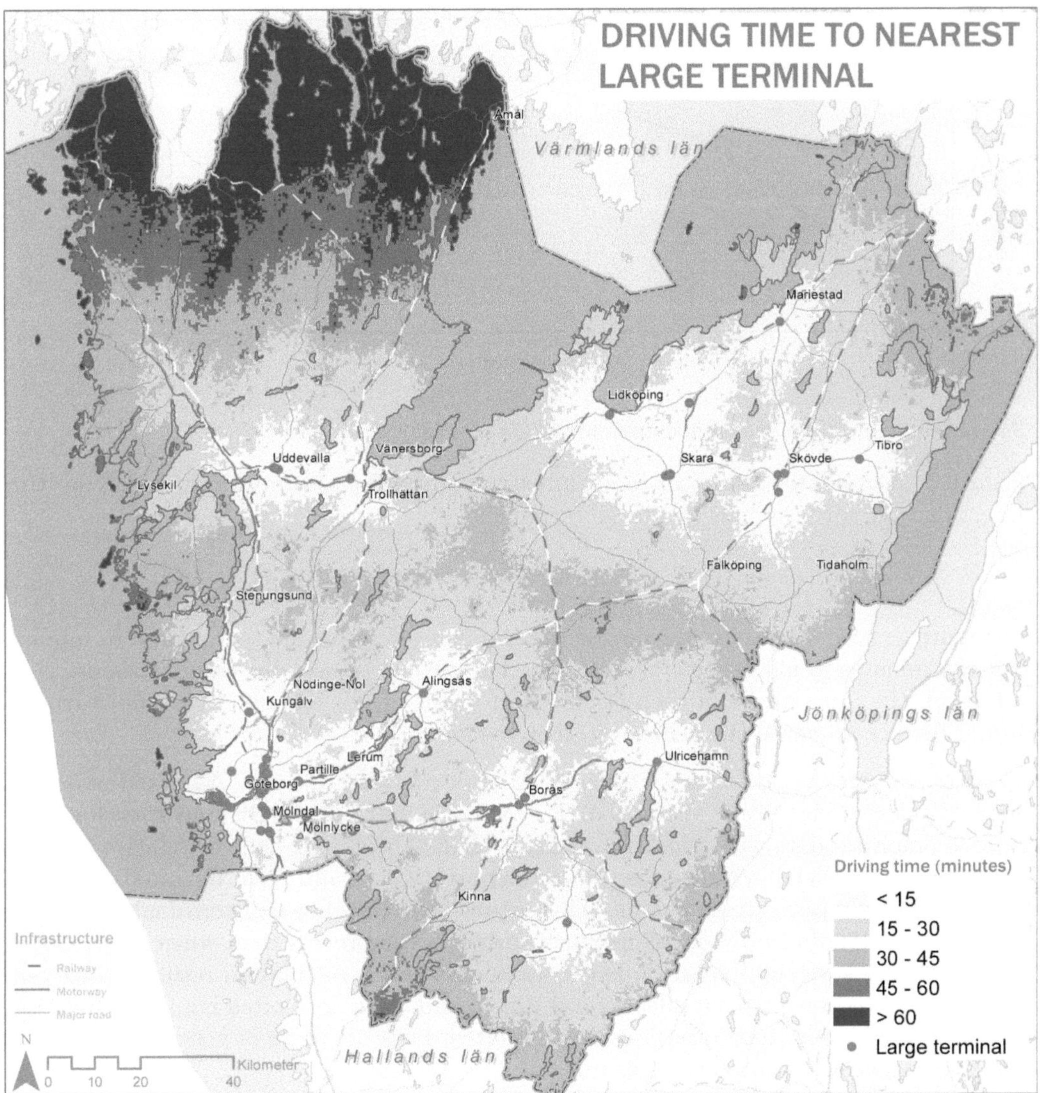


Figure 4: Accessibility in terms of driving time to the nearest large terminal, defined as having annual turnover exceeding SEK 100 million

equally valuable regardless of driving time. A terminal located a 60-minute drive away from the starting point is given the same value as a terminal located 5 minutes from the customer. Again, it is important to set driving time and distance parameters based on empirical data, to reflect real behaviour as well as possible.

Transferring the concept of travel behaviour to freight transport is complex, since the choice of route or terminal is usually not determined by the driver, but instead results from the commercial need to transport a product. The choice of starting point (e.g., firm) and destination point (e.g., terminal) then depends on several factors, such as business arrangements limiting what terminals to use and goods requiring special treatment (e.g., frozen foods). This brings the discussion to the question of constructing weights for destinations and travel distance to model accessibility more realistically.

### 4.4  Weighed measures

Some form of weighting is traditionally used in transport models (de Dios Ortúzar, Willumsen 2011) to create better theoretical approximations of actual travel behaviour. Destinations located farther away then become more costly to reach, while the more important the destination is, the more attractive it becomes. Translated into the terms

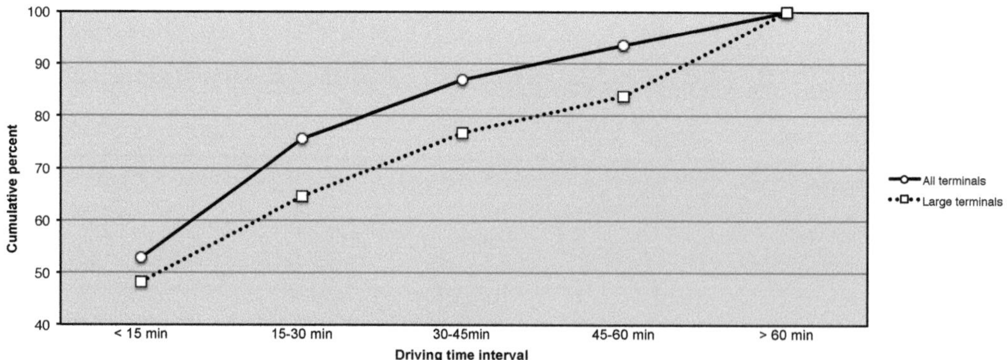


*Source*: authors' calculations; firm data from GILDA

Figure 5: Cumulative share of food industry companies within different driving-time intervals from all terminals and large terminals

of Figure 3, accessibility would not be determined solely by the travel time in minutes, but the minutes would become "longer" the farther one travels due to distance decay. In addition, the importance of each terminal in terms of, for example, size and turnover, would further influence the degree of attractiveness.

However, this approach has at least two important limitations. As noted above, we currently know very little about the "travel behaviour" of freight and therefore have limited empirical data with which to weight both distance decay and the relative influence of destinations. What we know is that transportation to and from terminals is part of increasingly complex supply chains. This means that the choice of terminal for a single shipment is determined by decisions much earlier in the process than when the transport is performed. A second limitation is the usefulness of the calculation results. Since both the distance and target point affect travel time based on various often nonlinear functions, the end result cannot be interpreted in minutes; instead, there is a need to construct relative weighted accessibility measures.

Figure 7 illustrates the driving time to the nearest terminal weighted by the terminals' annual turnovers. The weights are set using a simple linear logic in order to clearly illustrate the effects of a weighted measure. Small terminals with large hinterlands clearly illustrate poor relative accessibility. These results indicate that choosing the nearest terminal is often unrealistic, as exemplified by the two terminals located in Götene (see inset map in Figure 7). The southern terminal has a high turnover and is therefore favourably weighted, while the northern terminal has a considerably lower weight. In practice, there is only 1 minute of driving time between the two terminals, so all potential customers in the northern area of very extensive "weighted travel time" can easily choose the southern option instead. One method to solve the problems associated with treating the nearest terminal as the default would be to calculate the travel time to the nearest two or three terminals. A problem with this approach would arise in areas with very few terminals where the second or third terminal could be located very far away.

It is also possible to use weighting in analysing potentials at different locations. Figure 8 illustrates this with a calculation of accessibility weighted by terminal turnover, where higher turnover implies a higher potential service level. The map shows the aggregated total terminal turnover accessible within 60 minutes of driving time. The actual aggregated values for highly accessible areas become astronomical, obviously with no connection to the real values of points in the region. The advantage of this measure is that it qualifies the differences between areas with many terminals in absolute terms, but differing greatly in size. The pattern in Figure 8 does not differ significantly from that in Figure 6, but the values are much more dispersed and thus highlight the significance of being nearer large facilities, rather than just any facility.

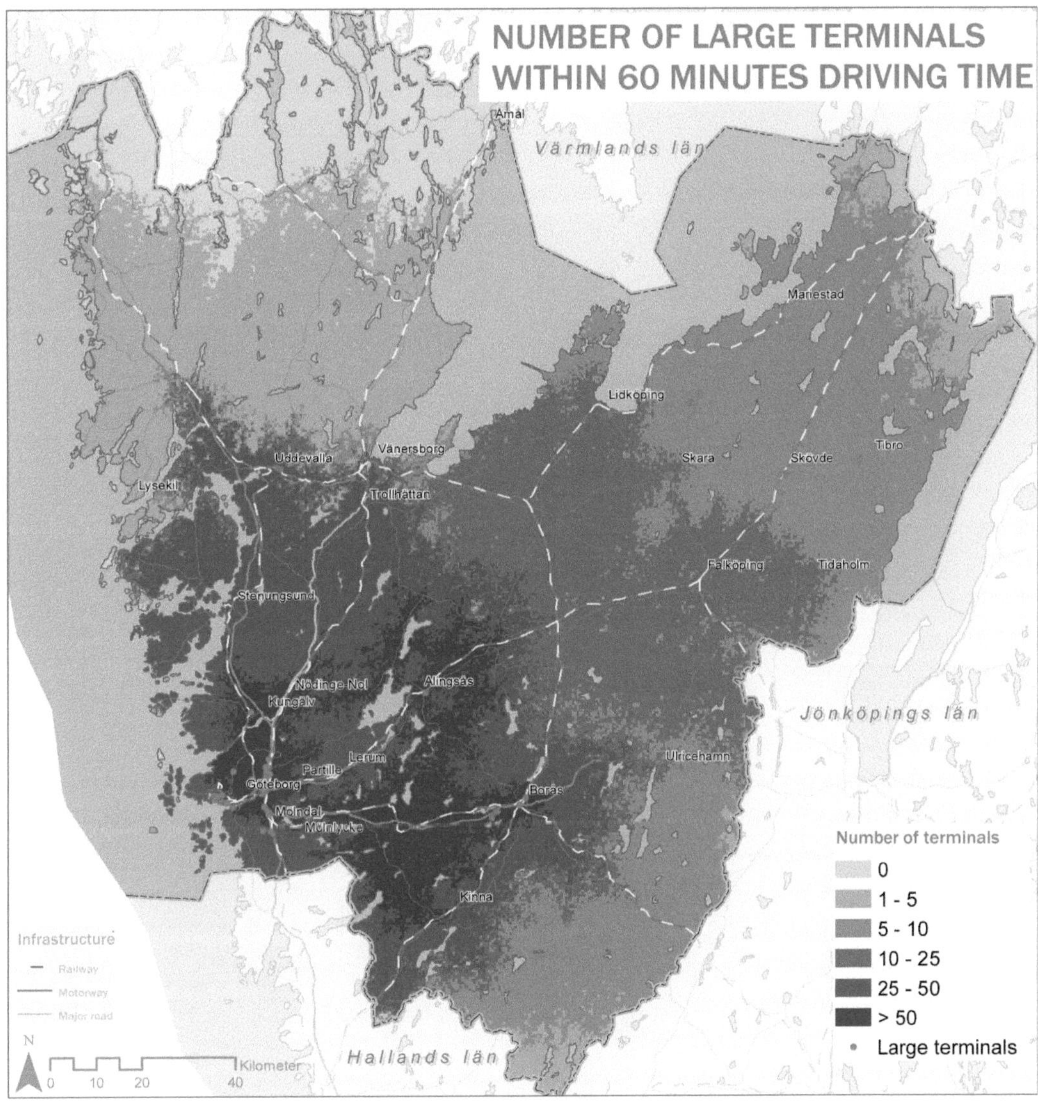


Figure 6: Number of large terminals accessible within 60 minutes of driving time

### 4.5 Spatial aggregation of detailed measures

Analysis and measures have so far been visualized with a spatial resolution of 500 metres.
This resolution shows intra-regional variations very well, but is less suitable for follow-up
at the national level. Since national targets are already using municipalities as the spatial
unit for monitoring transport policy objectives, we propose using a method of spatial
aggregation and combining measures into one single composite measure. The following
exercise should be regarded as an example for discussion, rather than as a complete and
finished measure ready for application.

The starting point for the measure will be the municipality. The first step is to
assign a centre point to each municipality where trips start or finish depending on the
measure. We suggest that centre points should be calculated based on the spatial pattern
of logistics-sensitive industry. In this case, the weighted centre point for the food industry
is our proxy for logistics-intensive industry.

We then select three measures meant to complement each other:

1. *Terminal proximity*: driving time from the municipal centre to the nearest terminal
   weighted by the terminal's economic turnover – This measures the extent to which
   the municipality has large terminal capacity in its immediate vicinity.

2. *Terminal potential*: the sum of the terminal's financial turnover earned within 60

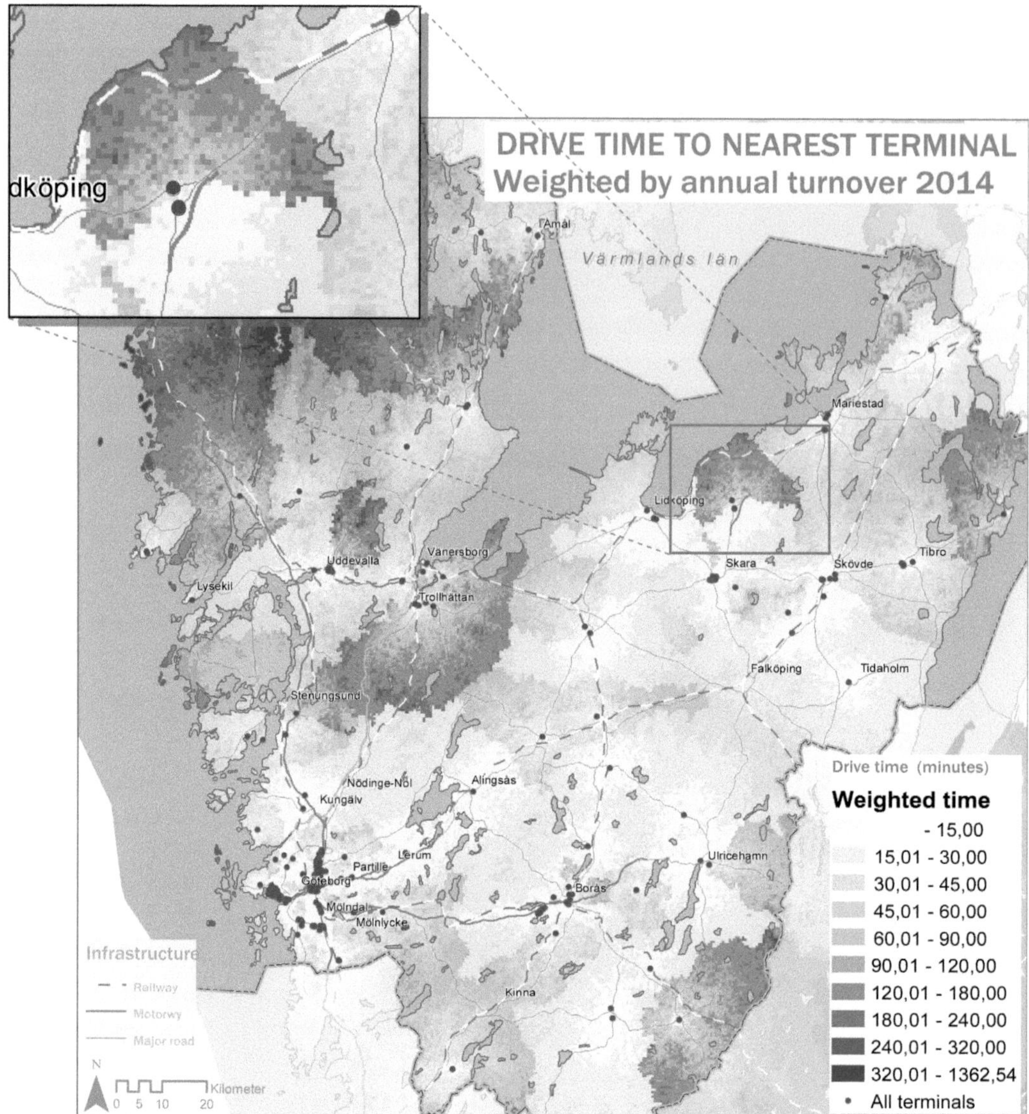


Figure 7: Accessibility measured as driving time to nearest terminal, weighted by annual turnover of terminal

minutes of driving time from the municipal centre – This complements terminal proximity and indicates the potential attractiveness of the area for the localization of logistics-intensive businesses.

3. *Road/Rail combination potential*: the total weighted value of the size of intermodal terminals reachable within 60 minutes of driving time from the municipal centre – This indicates the potential accessibility of good combined transport opportunities.

Each indicator is mapped in Figure 9. Indicator 1, the proximity indicator, produces more heterogeneous results than do the cumulative potential indicators illustrated in the two other maps. Accessibility is very good in the Gothenburg metropolitan region and along the major transport corridors. Also apparent are single peripheral municipalities each with a large terminal.

Indicator 2 reflects the dominance of the Gothenburg region due to the concentration of large terminals there. Again, note that the maps include only terminals located in Västra Götaland County, putting outlying municipalities at a relative disadvantage. Indicator 3 clearly shows the importance of Gothenburg; this particularly applies to the large multimodal terminals in the port, which weigh heavily in this context.

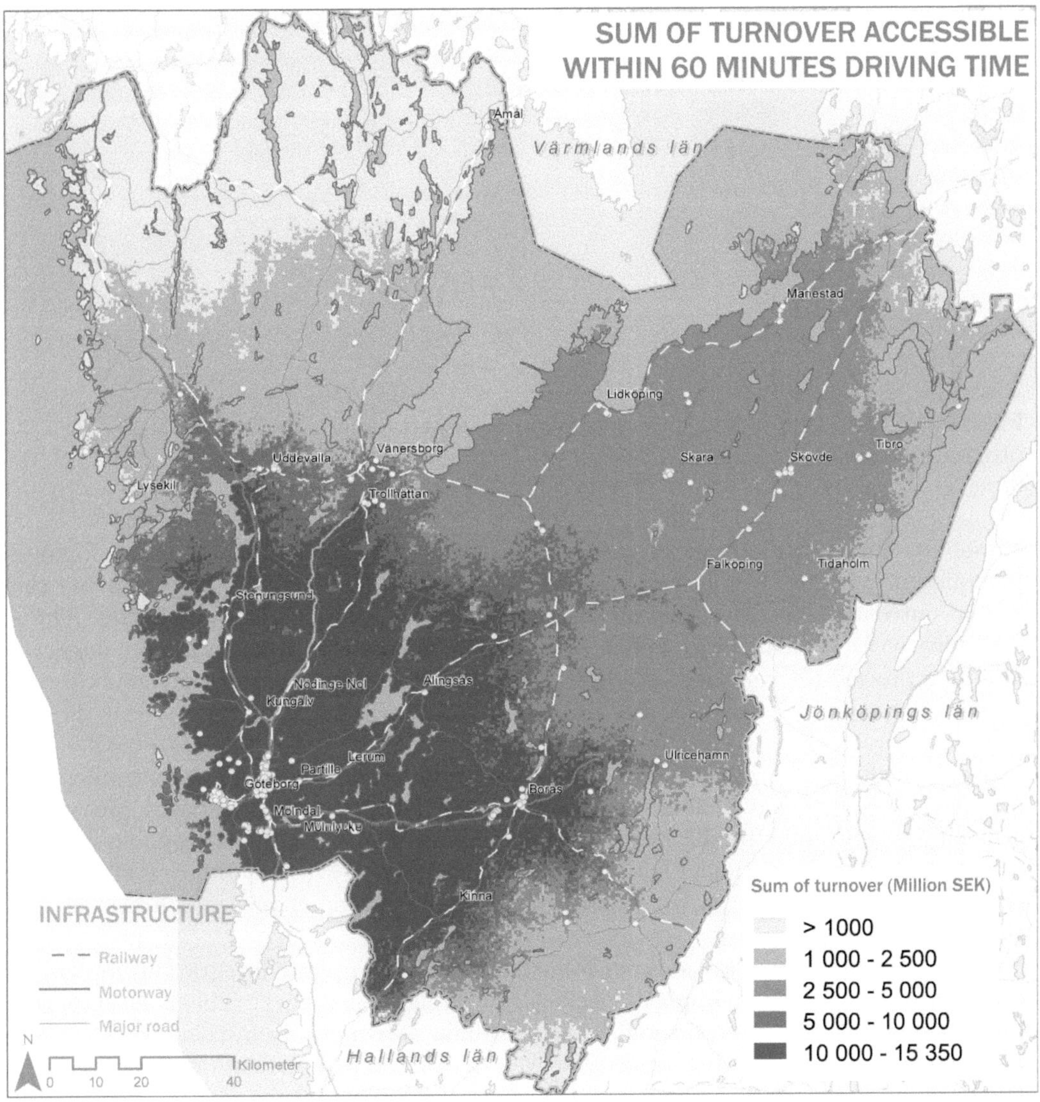


Figure 8: Aggregated terminal turnover accessible within 60 minutes of driving time

The measures are relatively straightforward in that they are related to driving time measured in minutes. However, merging the three indicators into one is problematic since they are weighted differently and their numerical outputs differ greatly. One way to achieve this would be to calculate the share of each municipality based on the total of the region and then add the relative numbers. Another method would be to rank all the municipalities for each indicator and then merge the three ranking figures to form a common ranking score. This method will be used here based on the simplicity of communicating and follow-up over time.

Figure 10 shows the summary score per municipality, illustrating how the major transportation corridors in the region have better access to logistics services than do their neighbouring municipalities. It is also very clear how proximity to the county's main urban centre of Gothenburg exerts an influence. One can see an inner and an outer ring of municipalities with very good accessibility located around Gothenburg.


## 5   Discussion

The main advantage of the accessibility concept in freight transport planning and policy lies in its integration of transportation and land use. Current approaches often focus on just one of the two. Transport planning is mostly concerned with network-related aspects

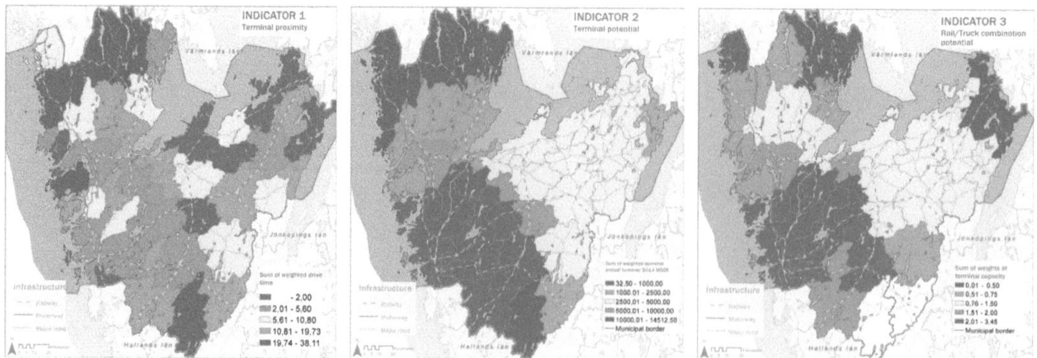

Figure 9: Illustration of the three municipality-based indicators. Left to right: terminal proximity, terminal potential, and rail/truck combination potential

of mobility efficiency such as speed, connectivity, flows, congestion, and parking. Land-use planning, in contrast, traditionally addresses issues related to human activities and their spatial outcomes, such as housing, economic development, and leisure activities. The accessibility concept offers a way to link these fields, taking a step towards a more integrated planning process (Bertolini 2005). It supports the link between transport/mobility and social sustainability issues (Lucas 2012), since changes in mobility always have different spatial accessibility outcomes for different groups in society. Being able to combine two areas of planning into one also entails potential problems. Obviously, an extra degree of complexity results when dealing with transport and land use simultaneously. Measures of accessibility will undoubtedly be more multi-dimensional than, for example, population density or traffic flows. There is also an added component when evaluating accessibility change over time, since both transportation and land use can change simultaneously over the same period.

Given the potential for the accessibility approach to support integration in planning, how can this approach be applied specifically to freight transport? This is an important question since freight and personal transport differ substantially in this respect. Unlike personal transport, freight transport is driven by derived commercial demand emanating from the business sector. Choice of transport mode or route is the combined result of a logistics chain comprising several frequently conflicting dimensions, such as cost, reliability, and scale economies. Accessibility in freight transport is much more likely to be a business matter, while in personal transport it directly mirrors the potentials of individuals and their everyday lives in different locations. Having this distinction in mind is important when asking questions about accessibility levels, for whom and where. On the other hand, accessibility measures may also be used with specific planning questions in mind, to understand how different groups in different places are, for example, influenced by new investment in logistics terminals and infrastructure.

Even a basic travel-time map provides a wealth of information. The use of "real time" measured in minutes without weighting or model calculations constitutes a potentially powerful outcome due to ease of interpretation: no expert knowledge is needed to conclude that ten minutes is twice as long as five minutes. This makes simple accessibility measures useful tools in communication between professional groups, such as planners and logistics business representatives, as well as with the general public in matters of spatial planning to promote more sustainable and inclusive urban regions. This is not to argue that accessibility should replace other well-proven methods. However, as an additional approach, it provides views that might foster more informed debate and ultimately better decisions.

Based on the data collection and accessibility mapping exercise described here, several key strengths and limitations can be identified. Data availability and quality is the major area of concern. However, specific institutional and business issues relating to the freight transport sector are also important, as are questions regarding the context in which accessibility measures are being used. Each of these areas will be discussed below.

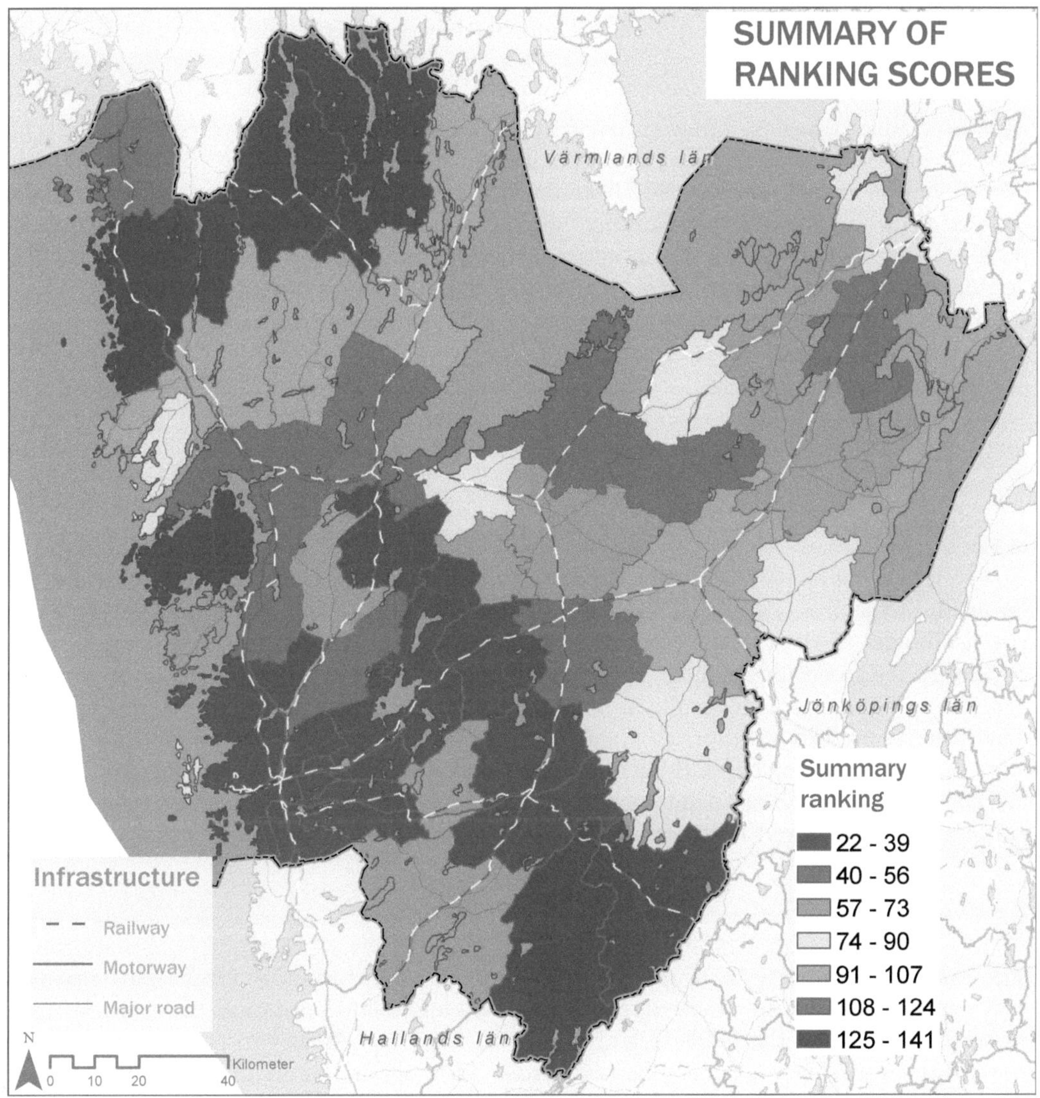


Figure 10: Illustration of the summary ranking scores per municipality

The single most pressing concern is data access and quality. Constructing useful measures of accessibility for freight transport calls for information about points of supply and demand and their locations. Since the industry encompasses a vast array of goods and destinations, it is insufficient to identify just any terminal or any customer. A basic need is business sector information in order to identify customer segments and terminal functions and to discern service levels.

The terminal data for the example maps shown here were produced in two stages. First, an automated search script scanned the official national company register (WSP 2013). Second, this was followed by a time-consuming manual check by the authors, resulting in a 25% increase in the number of terminals, many reclassifications, and the identification of multiple counting of the same terminal used by different companies. We estimate that officially available firm-level data are insufficiently reliable for accessibility analysis without considerable manual updating, possibly supported by enhanced models for the automated searching of business registers.

Specific surveys offer a potential way forward. In the case of freight transport, there is a lack of open statistical data on how goods actually flow, who is transporting goods, and what kinds of goods these are. This information is central to building more advanced models of accessibility in which the "travel behaviour" of the goods is taken into account. The assumption that the nearest terminal is the one selected is unrealistic, as indicated by current projects collecting detailed information on freight flows (see Dablanc 2013, Giuliano et al. 2015).

The question of terminal access is related partly to data availability and partly to logistics chain strategies. Many transport terminals are integrated into company-internal flows of material. For example, large retail chains or manufacturing firms employ their own global high-precision logistics systems with large warehouses. These are unavailable to local firms and should therefore not be part of an accessibility analysis of the general potentials of a specific area. From a local land-use planning perspective, however, these activities contribute to both employment and negative environmental effects.

The resolution of the maps in this study is very high. Results are presented using 500-metre cells across the region, which has proven very useful for planning problems at the local and regional scales (Elldér, Larsson 2011). However, this resolution is too high for following up policies and investments at the national level: technical limitations restrict the handling of large datasets, and complementary data are lacking at such a detailed level.

Finally, we would like to emphasize the user side of accessibility measures. So far most of the discussion has been from the producer side, focusing on measures, data, and output. However, if a non-expert user such as a planner or politician cannot fully understand the maps and measures, there is a significant communication problem that seriously limits the usefulness of these tools (te Brömmelstroet 2010). This exemplifies a wider issue regarding the sometimes contradictory relationship between scientifically sound models and the usefulness of their results in non-expert environments. The desire to model reality has often resulted in attempts to create big models that quickly become so complex that their outcomes cannot be used without expert knowledge (Lee 1973, Geertman, Stillwell 2004). This is not to say that modelling should be abandoned, but we would like to emphasize the user and the context in which results are implemented.

## 6    Conclusion

The use of accessibility measures to support policy and planning for freight transport and urban development offers a promising and long-needed potential for cross-sectoral integration between the fields of transport and land use. However, to fully exploit this potential several barriers must be overcome. This paper has identified a few problem areas, such as data availability and quality as well as the complexity and communicability of measures. Though these are definitely challenges in themselves, they are technical and relatively specific and can be addressed with a carefully devised research programme. Instead, we would like to highlight the wider and more complex policy and planning context for the application of accessibility analysis, especially potential tensions between actors and interests in the freight transport sector and its relations with society in general and urban development issues in particular.

While personal transport and accessibility can be related directly to individuals and their everyday activities as well as to society and planning on multiple scales, freight transport is primarily an activity organized by the private business sector. This has important implications for the usefulness of the accessibility concept and the methods of implementing it. Figure 11 illustrates this as two routes from an overall national policy objective towards more detailed planning objectives and implications in the private business and public realms. We are aware that the distinction between private and public is far from straightforward and binary; however, for reasons of clarity, we will pursue this division in the following discussion.

The point of departure is the black box in the centre of the figure containing the formulation of the overall national transport policy objective. In transport and land-use planning, this has predominantly been treated as the downward, stepwise application of national policy to regional and local levels of public planning. The more detailed the level, the further from the national goal and the more important the local context is, or should be, in terms of how to interpret and implement policies in a democratic and inclusive way. In contrast, if we follow the upward route, policies play a much more marginal role in the everyday running of businesses. Their main objective, emanating from commercial,

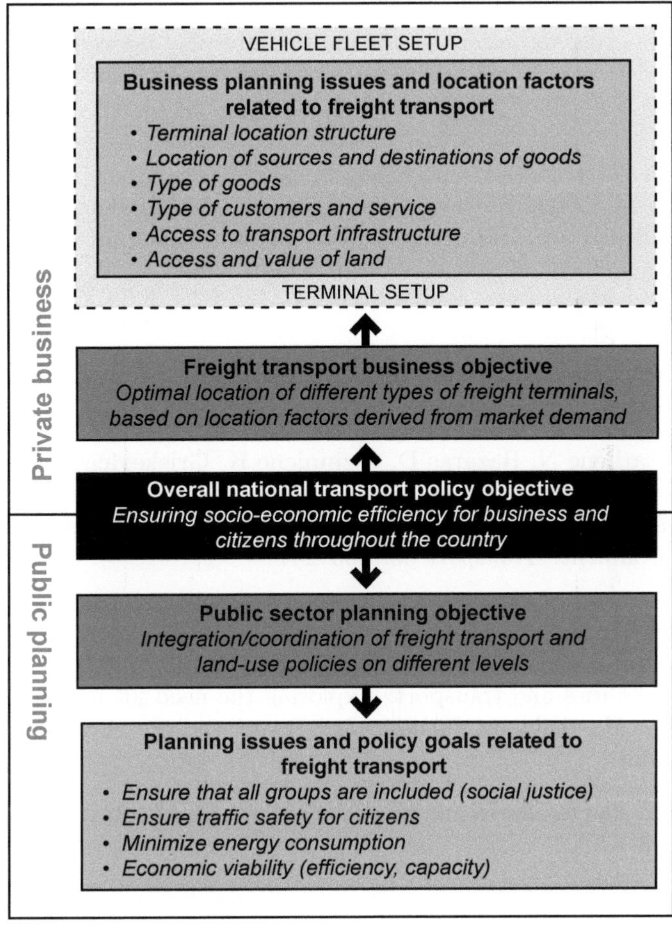



Figure 11: How the national transport policy objective can be implemented in the business and public planning spheres

market pressures, is to provide services that customers are prepared to pay for in order to earn a profit and meet the company's and shareholders' financial targets.

We might say that from the national policy objective, the scope and impact will widen downwards in the public planning sphere and narrow upwards in the business context. This is not to say that the two spheres are unconnected or exist in two parallel worlds, as urban planning is constantly interacting with freight transport and vice versa. However, accessibility analysis and accessibility questions affect the two spheres in different ways.

Imagine, for example, an expanding international port located in an expanding urban area. What would be the relevant accessibility question to ask in order to follow up the national goal? From a business competitiveness perspective, it might be interesting to know whether companies can access more and better logistics services over time in the region or whether more companies can reach the port within the same time as an effect of new infrastructure investment. For an urban planner or local policy maker in the same port city, the question of the accessibility of jobs, schools, and recreation for citizens might be at the top of the agenda. The same infrastructure that supports increased terminal and port accessibility could create physical barriers, including noise and pollution, that decrease the accessibility of other amenities for citizens.

The combination of transport and land-use components is the main strength of the accessibility concept. However, for its productive use we must be careful about its implementation context. The above example illustrates how different groups might have conflicting interests in the same space. To better measure and follow up urban transport land-use policies and potential conflicts, we must develop our knowledge, mainly about the private business sphere. The "travel behaviour" of goods and locational decision making in the freight sector are keys to implementing the accessibility concept as a long-needed integration tool in order to better understand the interplay between freight transport and its urban context.

## References

Allen J, Browne M (2008) Review of survey techniques used in urban freight studies. Transport studies group, University of Westminster, London

Banister D (2005) *Unsustainable Transport: City Transport in the New Century*. Routledge, London

Banister D (2008) The sustainable mobility paradigm. *Transport Policy* 15: 73–80. CrossRef.

Barysiene J, Batarliene N, Bazaras D, Ciziuniene K, Griskeviciene D, Griskevicius AJ, Lazauskas J, Maciulis A, Palsaitis R, Vasiliauskas AV, Vasiliene-Vasiliauskiene V (2015) Analysis of the current logistics and transport challenge in the context of the changing environment. *Transport* 30: 233–241

Berglund S (2001) GIS in transport modelling. Phd dissertation. Department of Infrastructure, Royal Institute of Technology, Stockholm, Sweden

Bertolini L (2005) Cities and transport: Exploring the need for new planning approaches. In: Albrechts L, Mandelbaum S (eds), *The network society: A new context for planning*. Routledge, Oxford

Breheny M (1978) The measurement of spatial opportunity in strategic planning. *Regional Studies* 12: 463–479. CrossRef.

Dablanc L (2013) Commercial goods transport, Paris, France. Case study prepared for global report on human settlements 2013 http://www.unhabitat.org/grhs/2013

Dablanc L, Ross C (2012) Atlanta: a mega logistics center in the Piedmont Atlantic Megaregion. *Journal of Transport Geography* 24: 432–42. CrossRef.

David PD (2015) Factors affecting municipal land use cooperation. *Land Use Policy* 42: 170–182. CrossRef.

de Dios Ortúzar J, Willumsen LG (2011) *Modelling Transport*. John Wiley & Sons, Chichester. CrossRef.

Elldér E, Ernstson U, Fransson U, Larsson A (2012) Analysverktyg för tillgänglighetsberäkning med bil och kollektivtrafik i Västra Götaland. Slutrapport. occasional papers 2012:1. Department of Human and Economic Geography, University of Göteborg, Göteborg, Sweden

Elldér E, Gil Solá A, Larsson A (2012) Spatial inequality and workplace accessibility. *Environment and Planning A* 44: 2295–2297

Elldér E, Larsson A (2011) Improving regional transport accessibility planning. A GIS-based methodology based on micro-level register data. Regional Studies International Conference. 18-20 April 2011. Newcastle upon Tyne, UK

Evans I (1977) The selection of class intervals. *Transactions of the Institute of British Geographers* 2[1]: 98–124. CrossRef.

Ferreira A, Beukers E, te Brömmelstroet M (2012) Accessibility is gold, mobility is not: A proposal for the improvement of transport-related Dutch CBA. *Environment and Planning B* 39: 683–697

Geertman S, Stillwell J (2004) Planning support systems: an inventory of current practice. *Computers, Environment and Urban Systems* 28: 291–310. CrossRef.

Geurs K, Ritsema van Eck J (2001) Accessibility measures: review and applications. Rivm report 408505 006. Netherlands National Institute of Public Health and the Environment, Bilthoven, The Netherlands

Geurs K, van Wee B (2004) Accessibility evaluation of land-use and transport strategies: review and research directions. *Journal of Transport Geography* 12: 127–140. CrossRef.

Giuliano G, Dablanc L, Rodrigue J, Seo S (2015) Building the database. Final report project no.: 15-1A. metroFreight Center of Excellence, University of Southern California, Los Angeles, California, USA

Handy S (2002) Accessibility- vs. mobility-enhancing strategies for addressing automobile dependence in the U.S. European Conference of Ministers of Transport, Brussels

Hansen WG (1959) How accessibility shapes land use. *Journal of the American Institute of Planners* 25: 73–76. CrossRef.

Haugen K (2012) The accessibility paradox. Gerum 2012:1. Department of Geography and Economic History,University of Umeå, Umeå, Sweden

Haugen K, Holm E, Strömgren M, Vilhelmson B, Westin K (2012) Proximity, accessibility and choice: A matter of taste or condition? *Papers in Regional Science* 91: 65–84. CrossRef.

Haugen K, Vilhelmson B (2013) The divergent role of spatial access: the changing supply and location of service amenities and service travel distance in Sweden. *Transportation Research A* 49: 10–20. CrossRef.

Hesse M (2008) *The City as a Terminal. The Urban Context of Logistics and Freight Transport*. Ashgate, Aldershot

Hägerstrand T (1970) What about people in regional science? *Regional Science Association Papers* XXIV: 7–21. CrossRef.

Ingram DR (1971) The concept of accessibility: A search for an operational form. *Regional Studies* 5: 101–107. CrossRef.

Jiang B (2013) Head/tail breaks: A new classification scheme for data with heavy-tailed distribution. *The Professional Geographer* 65[3]: 482–494. CrossRef.

La Paix L, Geurs K (2016) Train station access and train use: a joint stated and revealed preference choice modelling study. In: Geurs K, Patuelli R, Ponce Dentinho T (eds), *Accessibility, equity and efficiency: Challenges for transport and public services*. Edward Elgar Publishing, Cheltenham. CrossRef.

Larsson A, Elldér E, Vilhelmson B (2014) Accessibility atlas to analyse regional accessibility to labour in the food sector. In: Brömmelstroet M, Silva C, Bertolini L (eds), *Assessing usability of accessibility instruments*. Report 2 from the COST Action TU1002, European Science Foundation and the COST Office, Brussels

Lee DBJ (1973) A requiem for large scale models. *Journal of the American Institute of Planners* 39: 163–178. CrossRef.

Lindström A (2007) Territorial governance in transition. *Regional and Federal Studies* 17: 499–508. CrossRef.

Lucas K (2012) Transport and social exclusion: Where are we now? *Transport Policy* 20: 105–113. CrossRef.

McKinnon A (2009) The present and future land requirements of logistics activities. *Land Use Policy* 26: 293–301. CrossRef.

Melo MT, Nickel S, Saldanha-da Gama F (2009) Facility location and supply chain management – A review. *European Journal of Operational Research* 196: 401–412. CrossRef.

Ministry of Enterprise and Innovation (2011) Framtidens citylogistik. Rapport från arbetsgruppen för citylogistik inom Logistikforum. Näringsdepartementet, Stockholm, Sweden

Newman P, Kenworthy J (2015) *The End of Automobile Dependence. How Cities are Moving Beyond Car-Based Planning.* Island Press, Washington DC

Olsson J, Larsson A (2016) Accessibility to terminals in Västra Götland – A pilot study. PM 2016:9, Transport Analysis, Stockholm (in Swedish) http://www.trafa.se/-globalassets/pm/pm-2016_9-tillganglighet-till-terminaler-i-vastra-gotaland--en-pilot-studie.pdf

Olsson J, Woxenius J (2012) Location of freight consolidation centres serving the city and its surroundings. *Procedia – Social and Behavioral Sciences* 39: 293–306. CrossRef.

Olsson J, Woxenius J (2014) Localisation of freight consolidation centres serving small road hauliers in a wider urban area: barriers for more efficient freight deliveries in Gothenburg. *Journal of Transport Geography* 34: 25–33. CrossRef.

Páez A, Scott DM, Morency C (2012) Measuring accessibility: positive and normative implementations of various accessibility indicators. *Journal of Transport Geography* 25: 141–153. CrossRef.

Rodrigue J, Comtois C, Slack B (2013) *The Geography of Transport Systems.* Routledge, Abingdon

Sakai T, Kawamura K, Hyodo T (2015) Locational dynamics of logistics facilities: Evidence from Tokyo. *Journal of Transport Geography* 46: 10–19. CrossRef.

Sheffi Y (2012) *Logistics Clusters. Delivering Value and Delivering Growth.* MIT Press, Cambridge

SOU – Statens Offentliga Utredningar (2008) Vägen till ett energieffektivare Sverige. Slutbetänkande av Energieffektiviseringsutredningen, SPU 200:110

Straatemeier T (2008) How to plan for regional accessibility? *Transport Policy* 15: 127–137. CrossRef.

Swedish Transport Administration (2013) Godskartläggning i VG. Rapport 2013:151. Trafikverket, Borlänge

te Brömmelstroet M (2010) Equip the warrior instead of manning the equipment: Land use and transport planning support in the Netherlands. *Journal of Transport and Land Use* 3: 25–41

Transport Analysis (2013a) Indikatorer för en transportpolitisk måluppföljning – hur tillgänglighet påverkar konkurrens- och utvecklingskraft. Rapport 2013:2. Trafikanalys, Stockholm, Sweden

Transport Analysis (2013b) Indikatorer för en transportpolitisk måluppföljning – hur tillgänglighet påverkar konkurrens- och utvecklingskraft. Trafikanalys: Stockholm, Sweden

Transport Analysis (2013c) Transportarbete 1950-2012. *Trafikanalys: Stockholm, Sweden.* *http://www.trafa.se/sv/Statistik/Transportarbete/*

WSP (2013) Methodology for the identification of freight terminals in Sweden. Internal report (in Swedish). WSP, Stockholm, Sweden

# REGION

The Journal of ERSA
Powered by WU

Volume 4, Number 1, 2017, 17–30
DOI: 10.18335/region.v4i1.102

journal homepage: region.ersa.org

# Analysis of Freight Trip Generation Model for Food and Beverage in Belo Horizonte (Brazil)[*]

Leise Kelli de Oliveira[1], Rodrigo Affonso de Albuquerque Nóbrega[2], Daniel Gonçalves Ebias[3], Bruno Gomes e Souza Corrêa[4]

[1] Universidade Federal de Minas Gerais, Belo Horizonte, Brazil (email: leise@etg.ufmg.br)
[2] Universidade Federal de Minas Gerais, Belo Horizonte, Brazil (email: raanobrega@ufmg.br)
[3] Centro Universitário Formiguense, Formiga, Brazil (email: daniel_ebias@outlook.com)
[4] Universidade Federal de Minas Gerais, Belo Horizonte, Brazil (email: bgesc@hotmail.com)

Received: 20 November 2015/Accepted: 22 December 2016

**Abstract.** Today, one of the main challenges faced in urban logistics is the distribution of goods. In Brazil, mid to large cities have experienced negative consequences of unplanned urban sprawl as well as the lack of adequate transport infrastructure. As for the logistic standpoint, the relationship between urban planning and transportation planning must be better exploited towards the promotion of quality of life, and economic and environmental sustainability. The attractiveness of urban activities that attract the movement of people and goods and other component elements of urban space should be investigated. The presence of bars and restaurants falls within this context and is therefore vital and responsible for a significant percentage of jobs and revenue in a city. This paper presents the results of a freight trip generation model developed for pubs and restaurants in Belo Horizonte (Brazil). The data for the freight trip generation model were obtained by survey. A structured questionnaire was designed to obtain information about goods, frequency, operational time, place of performance of the loading/unloading of goods, establishment size and the number of employees. In creating the proposed models, a simple linear regression was applied to correlate the following variables: (i) number of trips versus area of the establishment; (ii) number of trips versus number of employees; (iii) number of trips versus operation day of the establishment. With the results of the linear regression for trip generations, data interpolation was conducted based on the standard deviation of the results to define the sample classification bands. Finally, the resulting trip generation surface was analysed together with other geographic data such as demographic data, road network density and socioeconomic data. Findings indicate the importance of a mathematic-geographic model for trip generation as a feasible approach to support transportation planning & operation for urban goods distribution. Critical information such as the high concentration of pubs and restaurants in the same region can reinforce the vocation of the city for trading. However, an elevated number of freight vehicles to meet a high and growing demand becomes a problem especially in areas where the urban road network is not efficient (not properly designed and parking spaces not properly used). This study also highlights the need for an urban freight mobility plan and public policies, by offering sustainable alternatives for urban goods distribution,

[*]The support of the National Council for Scientific and Technological Development (CNPq) is acknowledged and appreciated. The authors thank the Municipality of Belo Horizonte for the database, which allowed the analysis of this study. The authors would also like to thank anonymous reviewers for the suggestions to improve this paper.

which improve the urban environment. By using geospatial analysis, the study delivered statistics data and maps to catch the attention of decision makers and transportation managers, therefore facilitating the discussion on transportation policies in the city of Belo Horizonte.

**Key words:** urban goods distribution, freight trip generation, trucking, pubs and restaurants, geospatial analysis, Brazil

## 1   Introduction

Nowadays, the distribution of urban goods is one of the main challenges faced by policy makers, transportation authorities and the private sector in Brazilian cities. These cities present mostly a pattern of non-organized growth, lack of planning, and especially a lack of adequate infrastructure. Other than these well known factors there is also an increasing rate of population density. According to the Brazilian Institute of Geography and Statistics (IBGE 2010), about 83.4% of Brazil's population lives in urban areas. Concomitantly to the lack of planning for the use of urban space, the increasing volume of vehicles is also aggravating the situation. The population growth in the city increases the demand for goods and services that potentiate the problems related to urban mobility and urban freight transport. According to Holguín-Veras et al. (2012), the relationship among land use and freight represents a central issue for adequately planning investments in infrastructure and land use policy. However, the current transportation planning process in Brazil does not estimate freight activity to assist decision makers, which is critical information to be considered when making infrastructure investment choices. This fact motivated the development of this study, which presents data and models to estimate the flow of urban freight vehicles.

In this context, we hypothesize in this investigation that a transportation model sensitive to geographic-based context will add quality and efficiency to computing freight trip generation by considering local characteristics. Thus, this paper's analysis of a freight trip generation model was computed based on a survey developed for pubs and restaurants in the city of Belo Horizonte, Brazil. We analyse pubs and restaurants due to this sector's importance in Belo Horizonte (area of study); it represents 42% of the number of deliveries in the central Area (Oliveira 2014, Oliveira, Guerra 2014). Besides that, what makes this study distinct is its characterization of the sector and the geographical analysis of the results, which intends to inform transport policies for the distribution of food and beverage in pubs and restaurants. The methodology proposed in this study intends to provide a guideline for planning of urban freight transport in order to obtain data for freight transport policies through field surveys (this type of analysis is still incipient in the Brazilian context).

The paper is structured as follows: Section 2 provides a brief literature review on urban freight trip generation models in the Brazilian context; Section 3 describes the study area; Section 4 describes the methodology and data; results are illustrated in Section 5; and Section 6 concludes and discusses future research.

## 2   Brief notes about urban freight trip generation models

The estimation of freight trip generation is a critical component of traffic impact analyses (Holguín-Veras et al. 2013) and very important information to understand how goods move within an urban area. To Kulpa (2014, p. 197), freight trip generation refers to different areas or particular objects and may be estimated either by the number of vehicles (truck based model) or by the quantity of commodities measured in tons or values (commodity based model). Comi et al. (2012) also consider the delivery approach, which focuses on movements of goods measured in pick-ups and deliveries (delivery based model).

Brogan (1979) used trip rate per unit of area to understand the relationship between the number of truck-trips produced in/or attracted to an area, as well as the characteristics of that area. The author stated that the use of these rates contributes to the analysis of the impact of major truck-generating activities in certain sections of an urban area. An examination of the developed truck trip rates shows that, in general, commercial and industrial land uses are the largest generators of truck trips.

For Ogden (1992), understanding the relationship between transport and demand patterns is an essential component for modeling freight movement in urban areas. It evidences the link between movements of people and goods. Ogden (1992) also establishes a distinction between models based on movement of goods and models based on truck trips. In the model based on the movement of goods, producers and customers in a specific region create the demand for the movement of goods. Thus the movement of vehicles is a response to meet this demand. As a consequence, the truck trips establish a direct relationship with the movement of goods, and consequently the model outputs a certain amount of vehicle travel allocation. The author also developed models of attraction of products based on goods as well as on trips.

Tadi, Balbach (1994) estimated truck trips generated at warehouses, industrial sites, truck terminals and building areas using a regression model. Iding et al. (2002) developed a linear regression model that considers site area and number of employees as an alternative to the size of a business for each trip production and trip attraction per sector of industry.

Allen Jr. (2002) developed a demand forecast model to estimate the number of trips for medium and heavy trucks, considering the number of businesses and residences. Iding et al. (2002) present a freight trip model, obtaining attraction/production equations for different sectors, considering the area and the number of employees. Black (1999) developed similar study for Indiana-USA, considering 20 different products.

Comi et al. (2012) review the state-of-the-art on urban freight transport demand modelling and present different approaches after considering their pros and cons. One of the main conclusions of the authors is that the "direction relation between policies/measures and stakeholder's behaviours has not been investigated enough in the urban freight transport modelling literature" (Comi et al. 2012, p. 12). Anand et al. (2012) make a contribution to this gap, reviewing the literature concerned with urban freight modelling from the stakeholder's point of view describing their objective, descriptor choice and perspective towards the stakeholders' objective. Gonzalez-Feliu, Routhier (2012) analyze different models considering the function of the model, its scope and initial objectives, unit, model building approaches, choice of granularity and commercial applications and tools. An important conclusion of this review is about the relationship between goods flows and vehicle flows: if the focus is the impact of urban freight transport on urban traffic, the model unit must be considered vehicle-flows rather than commodity-flows which is commonly used in freight trip models. However converting commodity-flows to vehicle-flows is not a simple task (Gonzalez-Feliu, Routhier 2012). The authors claim that "modeling is not possible without knowledge of the existing situation, and in particular, knowledge about what is subject to change and what is invariable", so they suggest the development of procedures capable to understand the variation of data in space and time (Gonzalez-Feliu, Routhier 2012, p. 98).

Cherrett et al. (2012) indicate that 1.77 deliveries/week/100m$^2$ are transported in Winchester (UK). Using secondary data, Ducret, Gonzalez-Feliu (2016) attempt to connect a demand-estimation model and spatial modeling to evaluate the link between urban form characteristics and freight movements. The authors found that 2.9 deliveries/day are made by light commercial vehicles and 0.4 deliveries/day are made by single trucks, in Angers (France).

Holguín-Veras et al. (2016) discuss freight trip generation estimates. The authors indicate that "freight behavior research could be either a qualitative or a quantitative nature" (Holguín-Veras et al. 2016, p. 45). Priya et al. (2015) investigate an improved truck-trip model using time series, artificial neural networks and patterns of land-use.

With an innovative approach to model urban freight, Aditjandra et al. (2016) use a traffic survey and micro-simulation modeling to identify the impacts of freight deliveries and local service traffic at peak periods nearby the university campus in Newcastle (UK). The authors demonstrate that traffic surveys can be useful to assess the impacts of urban built environments on urban freight traffic. Sánchez-Díaz et al. (2016) propose a new set of variables that relate the establishment to its location, and assesses the

Table 1: Trip generation models to pubs and restaurants in Brazilian context

| Reference | Equation | Trips per establishment | Dependent variable | $R^2$ |
|---|---|---|---|---|
| Melo (2002) | $T = 1.333 + 0.0019A$ | 1.94 | Area | 0.797 |
| | $T = 2.963 + 0.0455A$ | | Area | 0.705 |
| Silva and Waisman (2007) | $T = 1.972 + 1.459E$ | - | Employers | 0.739 |
| | $T = 2.074 + 0.017A + 0.967E$ | | Area and Employers | 0.754 |

*Notes*: T ... Number of trips; A ... Area of establishment; E ... Number of employers

performance of novel explanatory variables on freight trip models. The results show that freight trip attraction is better modeled as a nonlinear function of employment and other geographic-based variables.

## 2.1 Urban freight models in the Brazilian context

Investigations of freight trip generation in the Brazilian context are incipient. There have so far been a few studies focused in São Paulo (Silva, Waisman 2007), Rio de Janeiro (Melo 2002, Gasparini 2008, Souza et al. 2010) and Campinas (Marra 1999). Marra (1999) developed a freight trip generation model designed for residential and commercial areas, based on the monthly freight flow. The model considers the area, the number of employees or residents and the average income per capita in the area as dependent variables. Melo (2002) developed an urban freight trip model for the city of Rio de Janeiro that considers groceries, clothing, retail stores, pubs and restaurants, construction material and fuel.

In particular, the sector of foods and beverages (focus of this paper) is a critical segment responsible for jobs, revenue and social activities vital to maintaining the economic sustainability of a city. Pubs and restaurants constitute a substantial volume of trips by attracting the movement of people and goods. Melo (2002) found 1.94 trips per day for establishments with an area between 60 and 780 square meters. Silva, Waisman (2007) developed a study that determined the freight trip generation rate for pubs and restaurants to a specific district in the city of Sao Paulo. The authors conducted a survey through a questionnaire for thirty establishments and collected information on daily freight trip rates, area of the establishment (in square meters) and number of employees. The authors identify the correlation between variables using multiple linear regressions. Gasparini (2008) developed a survey that analysed the freight trip rates for supermarkets and shopping malls in the city of Rio de Janeiro using the area, the number of customers, the number of parking spaces and the sales area as dependent variables in the model. The equations used in Brazilian freight trip studies to pubs and restaurants are presented in Table 1.

The approaches undertaken from the Brazilian context rely on the use of linear or polynomial regression and logarithm or exponential fit to determine the freight trip rates. Findings demonstrated a good fit ($R^2 \geq 0.7$), with wide divergences however, for the same variable as showed in Figure 1. Even with these good results, Souza et al. (2010) indicate the need for different equations or rates for different classes of goods and vehicles. This discussion demonstrates the complexity of the problem to be modelled and the importance of this topic of research.

The use of linear or polynomial regression as a methodology is a current trend, with Shin, Kawamura (2005), Bastida, Holguín-Veras (2009), Holguín-Veras et al. (2012), Holguín-Veras et al. (2013) and Priya et al. (2015) all using regression analysis to obtain a freight trip model. Sánchez-Díaz et al. (2016) incorporate locational variables and Aditjandra et al. (2016) use a traffic survey. The concept of locational variables is employed in the present study, which considers the importance of geographic-based information to evaluate which Brazilian model is more appropriate to estimate freight vehicle flows.

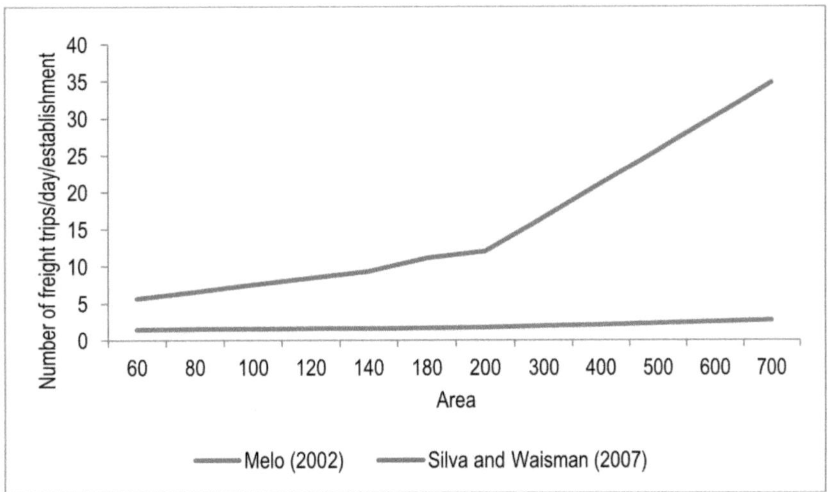


Figure 1: Graphical representation of Brazilian models to pubs and restaurants considering area as variable dependent

## 3 Study area and object of the investigation

This study focuses on the pubs and restaurants sector in Belo Horizonte city, which represents 42% of the number of deliveries in an area that contains the large majority of commercial establishments and urban mobility problems as well (Oliveira 2014, Oliveira, Guerra 2014). Belo Horizonte, founded in 1897 was planned to be the capital of the state of Minas Gerais. The plan envisioned a modern city that in 2010 could have a maximum population of 200,000 inhabitants living and working within the central boundary limited by Contorno Avenue (Oliveira et al. 2016).

Belo Horizonte has about 2.4 million inhabitants heterogeneously distributed over an area of 331 km$^2$. The city currently has the fourth largest Gross Domestic Product (GDP) of those in Brazil, with about 58.3 billion real (approximately currency rate: 1 euro is 3.60 real in October/2016). As a capital, commerce and public services are the key economic activities that propel the trading vocation of the city. The revenue comes mostly from services and commercial businesses, whereas the downtown area concentrates the federal, state and municipal governmental offices as well as an elevated number of commercial offices and industry headquarters. Belo Horizonte is surrounded by industrial-based cities and small towns mostly used as dormitory cities. The infrastructure of the capital's downtown makes it the most attractive area to retain hotels, restaurants, cafés and entertainment. This segment employs a substantial amount of jobs and makes an important contribution to the city's revenue.

In this investigation we hypothesize that a transportation model sensitive for geographic-based context will add quality and efficiency to computing freight trip generation by considering local characteristics. Thus, this paper analyses a freight trip generation model computed based on a survey developed for pubs and restaurants in the city of Belo Horizonte, Brazil. The distinctiveness of this study is the characterization of the sector and the geographical analysis of the results, which intends to inform transport policies for the distribution of food and beverage in pubs and restaurants. The methodology proposed in this study intends to provide a guideline for the planning of urban freight transport in order to obtain data for freight transport policies through field surveys (this type of analysis is still incipient in the Brazilian context).

## 4 Methodological approach

In theory, the data collection on movement of goods in an urban area can be obtained in different ways. In practice, however, because of the lack of waybill records or because of the nonexistence of registered information about trips, data about how, where the trips

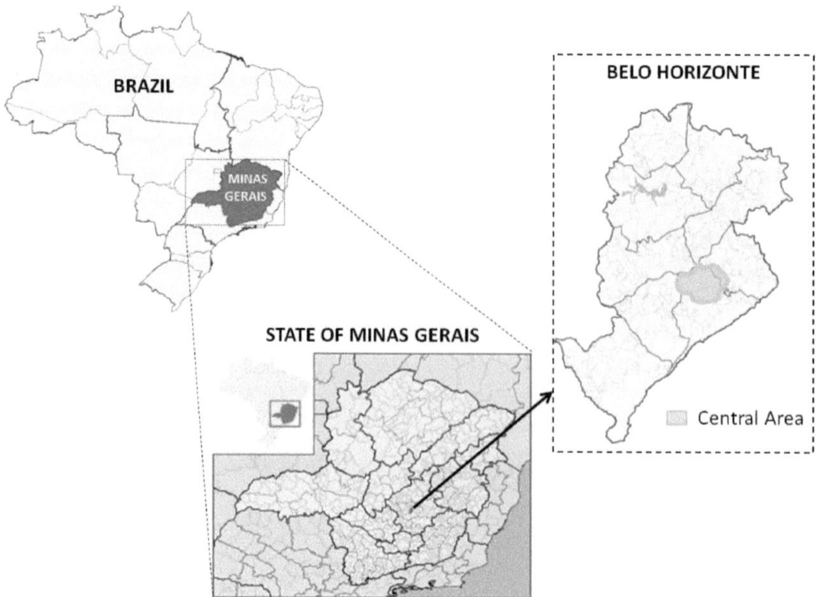


Figure 2: Geographic location of Belo Horizonte city and the study area

took place and about the volume of goods that flow in a city has been better obtained via survey. In this study we obtained data from specific stakeholders (retailers), based on interviews, as developed by Aditjandra et al. (2016). For the purposes of modeling urban goods, our data is categorized as vehicle/journeys (the route), as presented in Gonzalez-Feliu, Routhier (2012), and our model structure is defined as truck/vehicle as presented in Comi et al. (2012). These definitions are very important to characterize our methodology, which consists of:

1. develop a questionnaire to obtain freight flow data;

2. collect the data;

3. build and calibrate the model;

4. geographically analyse the results to understand the sector's impact on urban traffic.

### 4.1 Questionnaire

We developed a standard survey designed to obtain data that enables modeling of the vehicle journey categorized by foods and beverages. Table 2 presents the main information in the questionnaire. The questionnaire was validated with a pilot test in 10 commercial establishments and provides a database on the goods received in the establishments.

### 4.2 Data collection

The data collection was performed via interview. The interviews were conducted with the manager of the establishment or a technical staff member responsible for logistics operations. Unfortunately not all planned interviews were possible due to a lack of technical information, non-authorized personnel or when the establishment showed no interest in cooperating with the investigation.

The survey was conducted in 300 establishments. After the collection of data, the sample size was analyzed to determine the error and, for that, we used the simple random sample method. Other than information about the location of the pubs and restaurants, the interviewer also asked about desired and used routes, the time of the delivery and information about unload parking. Results are presented in Section 5.

Table 2: Main information of questionnaire

| Type of information | Detailed information |
| --- | --- |
| Information of establishment | Location <br> Name and function of interview <br> Telephone and mail |
| Characteristics of establishment | Foundation time <br> Day and working time <br> Area (square meter) <br> Number of employment |
| Receipt of goods | Origin of goods <br> Number of trucks by day of week <br> Time of delivery <br> Unload time |

### 4.3 Building and Calibrating the Model

The creation of the freight trip model presented in this paper was supported by a methodology developed by the Institute of Transportation Engineering (ITE 2008). Building a model requires a systematic comprehension of how data, tools methods and deliverables must be organized. Thus, the development of the model adds a methodological dimension for the approach, the data collection, the explanatory variables, the sampling elements and the date of the survey, that can be replicated in future investigations.

Besides the large number of variables and the complexity of the model for the development of the survey, it was also necessary to (ITE 2008):

- Consider the nature of the proposed model (type and size, geographical location, time/day that the model will be calibrated);

- Choose establishments that have characteristics that enables their travel demand to be modelled, such as:

  - it must be possible to reach an average rate of generation of trips with at least three elements;

  - it must be possible to use linear regression equations with six elements, but it is desirable to have at least 20 elements in the sample;

- Check the statistical correlation of the obtained model.

To define the model, we use linear regression. To validate the equations we use the coefficient of determination ($R^2$), which demonstrates how well an adjustment curve represents the relationship between the dependent and independent variables; the Student's t-test that determines the level of significance between the variables and the size of the sample; and the F-test that determines if the model is useful in predicting the flow. For this study, we considered valid the equations for which $R^2$ is greater than 0.5 (ITE 2008), ie, which represent 50% of the sample. In addition, we consider a confidence level of 95% for the t-test and significance level of 5% for the F-test. It is important to mention that models are best fit when $R^2$ is greater than 0.5, the sample size is greater than or equal to 4, and number of trips increases as the size of the independent variable increases (ITE 2008).

### 4.4 Geographical analysis

Once the trip generation model was computed, the establishments were located on the map by geocoding the addresses. We used Geographic Information System (GIS) tools to compute a continuous surface by interpolating the discrete values of travel per day delivered from the trip generation model. The method interpolates a raster surface from points using an inverse distance weighted (IDW) technique, which determines cell values using a linearly weighted combination of a set of sample points (travel per day per establishment). The weight is a function of inverse distance. The surface interpolated represents the dependent variable.

The interpolated surface represents the expected number of trips expanded to areas where sampling was not performed. Along with other maps, such as socioeconomics and transportation infrastructure, the spatial analysis helps to identify and understand the shortcoming and promotes a comprehensive standpoint for approaching the solution. For example, the solution can be applied to compute trip generation identifying areas with major demands of goods, therefore geographically correlating these areas with patterns of population income, age or behavior. This allows evaluation of the efficiency of the transportation policies that regulate urban distribution. As reported in Ducret, Gonzalez-Feliu (2016), which considered spatial categorization, urban freight modeling coupled to a GIS was used to demonstrate that spatial modeling can help organize logistics in the cities. In this work we aim to show the importance of integrating a robust freight trip generation model and GIS solution for providing an improved overview towards effective public policies for the city. Solutions in urban transportation planning must be addressed differently according to different aspects of population density and demand for goods.

## 5   Results and discussion

We used the Municipal Register of Taxpayers (MRT) provided by the Municipality of Belo Horizonte to know the total of establishments in the city. We identified 2,145 establishments as pubs, restaurants, juice houses or similar economic activity in this sector with the MRT database. We don't divide our sample and analyses in subcategories due to all establishments having similar characteristics: all commercialize food and drinks. Figure 3 shows the geographical dispersion of the selected establishments with high concentration in the 'Centro Sul' Region (59%). The 'Centro Sul' Region encapsulates the downtown area, and contains a large amount of jobs and a high density of residents, which compete daily for street use, parking spaces and mobility, therefore aggravating the problems of loading/unloading goods.

From the period July to August, 2014 we visited and interviewed three hundred establishments in the Belo Horizonte region. The sample has an error of 5.4% compared to the total amount of establishments, considering the simple random sample method. Our sample contains establishments with a building area of between forty-five and four hundred square meters, and with between one and thirty employees.

Our findings show that goods are delivered between five and six times a week in 66% of the establishments, except meat, fish and fresh food that have daily deliveries. The deliveries occur between 08:00 am and 10 am (71%). Beverages are delivered three to four times a week in 49% of the establishments, without a specific standard time for this kind of delivery. The peak day for deliveries is Tuesday (30%) followed by Friday (23%).

### 5.1   *Freight trip generation model*

After obtaining the data we applied the linear regression technique to correlate the dependent with the other independent variables. In this study, we considered as the dependent variable the number of freight trips and as the independent variable the area of the establishment and number of employees. We used the Pearson product-moment correlation coefficient to analyze the correlation between variables: when analyzing the number of freight trips and number of employees, , = 0.74 indicates a strong correlation between these variables. When considering number of freight trips and area of establishment; n = 0.70 also indicates a strong correlation between the variables. Using regression analysis to correlate the variables, we obtain results presented in Table 3. These models represent the number of daily freight trips (NT) attracted by establishments, considering area (A) and number of employees (E). It is necessary to multiply by a factor of 0.71 to determine the number of trips in peak hour (8am-10am).

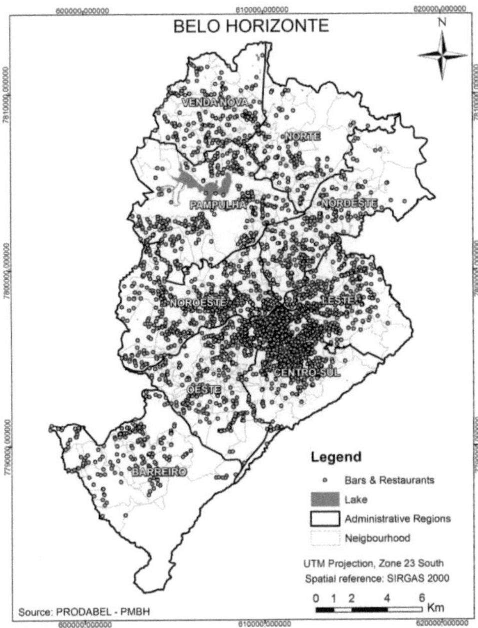

Figure 3: The geographical dispersion of Bars and Restaurants in Belo Horizonte

Table 3: Freight trip generation model to bars and restaurants

| Model | Equation | $R^2$ | T-Stat. | F-Test |
|---|---|---|---|---|
| Area (m$^2$) | NT = 0,98 + 0,0016A | 0.48 | 1.97 | 283 |
| | NT = 0,0076A | 0.81 | 1.97 | 1,339 |
| Employee | NT = 1,04 + 0,019E | 0.55 | 1.97 | 363 |
| | NT = 0,01E | 0.67 | 1.97 | 605 |
| Area (m$^2$) and Employee | NT = 1.01 + 0.014E + 0.00049A | 0.55 | 1.97 | 189 |

The models obtained are valid for establishments with:

- Area between 40 and 400 m$^2$;

- Number of employees between 1 and 30.

The statistical significance of the results was tested: the squared correlation ($R^2$) indicates that a minimum of 48% of the variability in the "number of freight trips" is explained by the "area". The best model correlates the "number of freight trips" and "area".

Figure 4 shows the comparison of the results of this study with other Brazilian models. The comparison indicates that the Silva and Waisman model estimates a large number of freight trips and has lower accuracy. The results found in this study are similar to the model presented by Melo. To check the accuracy of the model, we compare the real data with the model outputs. Considering the model that correlates area and the numbers of employees (model 3), the results are 0.4% overestimated than the real values.

Figure 5 shows the concentration of deliveries in Belo Horizonte, considering freight traffic to deliver goods in pubs and restaurants between 8am-10am. These findings, when combined with the situation of the urban transportation infrastructure and the current transportation policies, reveals an alarming scenario. According to the numbers, in this scenario 71% of the pubs and restaurants require their goods deliveries in a very short time. Thus, it is easy to picture that this scenario creates a large amount of vehicles competing for parking spaces and reducing flow efficiency of the streets.

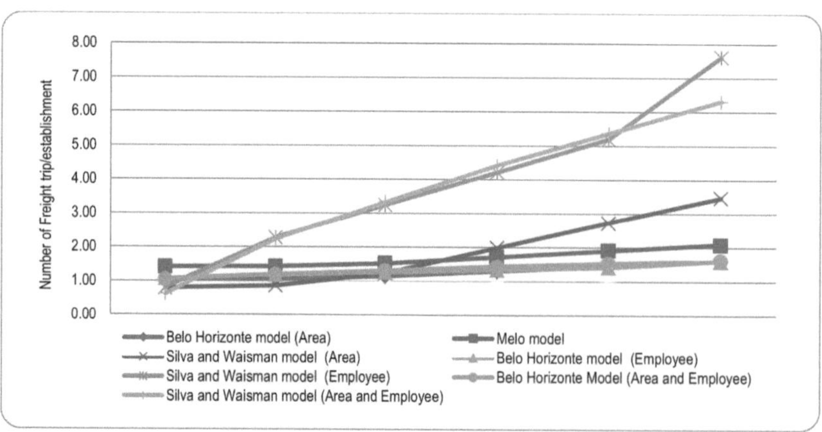



Figure 4: Comparison of models considering area (left) employers (center) and area and employees (right)

These results indicate the need for efficient public policies for urban freight transport. The pubs and restaurant sector is the only sector of the economy that generates a significant number of trips that overloads the transport infrastructure in these saturation times. Thus, the geographical analysis of results reinforces the results of the mathematical model and allows us to understand the extent of the problem.

## 5.2 Geographic overview of the model

The model provides an outstanding source for understanding the expected number of travels per business establishment. Based on this kind of information, urban planners and transportation managers can see and interact with indexes that reflect the demand for trip per business unit. However, the phenomena involved in the freight generation model includes a spatial component, which can be well explored if the geographic perspective is considered.

Transportation and economic development are areas intrinsically correlated in time and space. Therefore they rarely can be dissociated, especially when the goal of the study is to support public policies. For this reason, we introduced a basic structure, however realistic, for geographic analysis using the resulting model.

The model outputs the expected number of trips per day per establishment. The Municipal Register of Taxpayers data provides the addresses for the establishments. Together, these data were combined and displayed in a map. The surface provides the expected amount of trips per day for other regions in Belo Horizonte. It could be used, for example, to estimate trips per establishment for establishments that were not listed in the database or to provide an overview of the complex and delicate scenario of freight demand.

The geographic overview allows transportation and public managers to think about the freight in conjunction with other key factors that attract or repulse good deliveries in different regions of the city. Figure 6 illustrates a case scenario of downtown Belo Horizonte, which contains the majority of pubs and restaurants, a large amount of residents and a complex transportation network.

From the economic sustainability standpoint, there is an intrinsic relationship between population (consumers), foods and beverages (economic / social activity), mobility/accessibility to these services (existence of transportation infrastructure such as roads and public transportation) and the real demand for recharge supplies. The outputs of the model, when geographically spatialized and overlaid with other information provide an excellent perspective for supporting urban decision makers and policy makers.

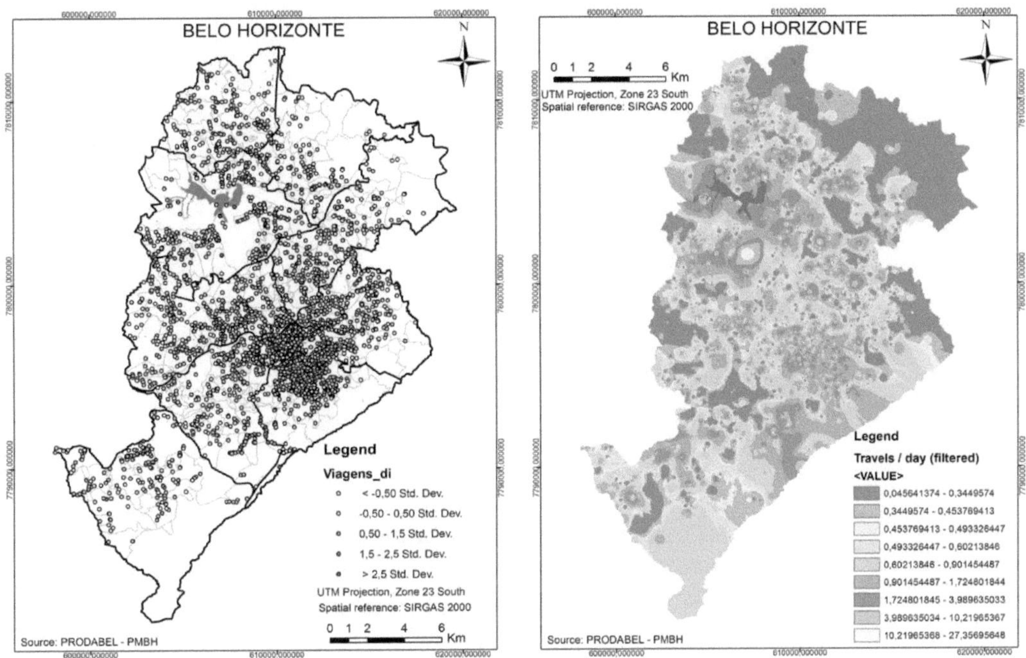


Figure 5: The geographical dispersion of deliveries to bars and restaurants in Belo Horizonte (left) and the surface of expected travel per day produced from the freight trip generation model (right)

### 5.3 Discussion of the results

The expected number of travels per day output from the model represents a realistic simulation of the current situation according to the survey from 2014. In order to better understand the results, the number of travels per day was loaded in a map containing the addresses of the establishments. This resulted in a punctual map (discrete information) that does not cover the whole area. Then, a geographic-based interpolation expanded the number of travels per day to a continuous surface as shown in Figures 5 and 6.

As shown in Figure 6, there is a geographic adherence between the number of travels per day, population and road density. The result indicates the need for an efficient urban freight policy to regulate the urban goods delivery towards meeting the demand of bars and restaurants.

As a recommendation, we draw attention to the importance of innovative ideas and alternative plans to lever positive changes in the urban transportation system to be presented and debated by specialists, authorities and the community. Holguín-Veras et al. (2016) suggest using forums and discussion groups to create a joint solution among the stakeholders involved in urban goods distribution. These measures highlight changes and can hopefully mobilize public managers, transportation managers and the population towards the continuous process of adaptation and improvement of public policies.

## 6 Conclusion

Regarding the development of this study, the key points are the characterization of an important economic sector of Belo Horizonte and especially the development of a freight trips generation model that is still an incipient theme in Brazil.

The model developed is mathematically robust and statistically acceptable. The model can be coupled to a GIS and provide results that support analysis in geographic contexts. We believe that the model can be used in the creation of public policies for Belo Horizonte: when we combine mathematical modeling with geographical analysis it is possible to understand the road occupancy impacts, and how and where the impacts will affect the population and economic sustainability of the region. These results can motivate the

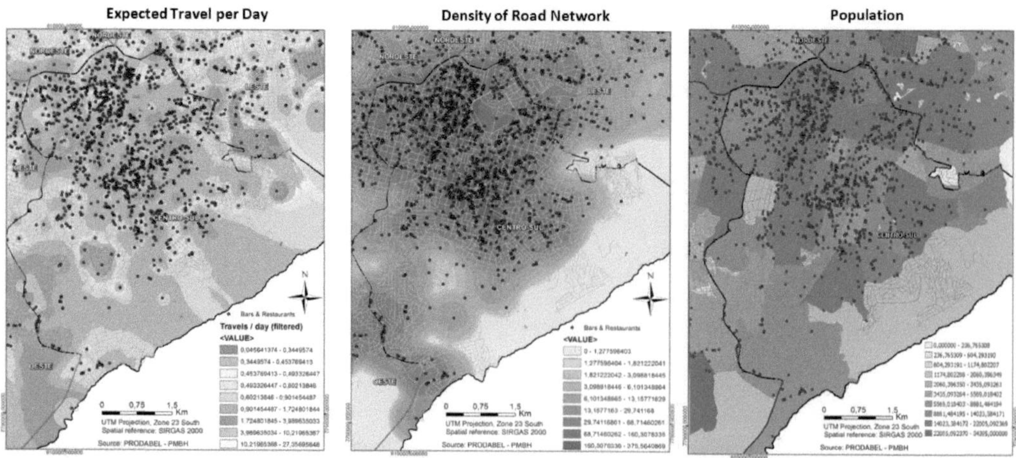

Figure 6: Overview of downtown Belo Horizonte using GIS maps used to improve the spatial analysis: the interpolated surface resulting from the trip generating model (left),the density of road network (center) and amount of population per neighborhood (right)

implementation of a less restrictive and more efficient public policy, to consolidate the goods and reduce the number of freight vehicles in urban areas.

The results of this study indicate differences between similar studies developed in Brazil. To do so, it demonstrates the necessity of the development of local models for freight demand management. Furthermore, the use of spatial analysis allows for the identification of potential sites for the implementation of this management policy, regarding the distances from main generators and attractors of freight trips.

## References


Aditjandra PT, Galatioto F, Bell MC, Zunder TH (2016) Evaluating the impacts of urban freight traffic: Application of micro-simulation at a large establishment. *European Journal of Transport and Infrastructure Research* 16: 4–22

Allen Jr. WG (2002) Development of truck models. Report prepared for Baltimore Metropolitan Council, Baltimore, MD

Anand N, Quak H, van Duin R, Tavasszy L (2012) City logistics modeling efforts: Trends and gaps – A review. *Procedia - Social and Behavioral Sciences* 39: 101–115. CrossRef.

Bastida C, Holguín-Veras J (2009) Freight generation models: Comparative analysis of regression models and multiple classification analysis. *Transportation Research Record* 2097: 51–61. CrossRef.

Black WR (1999) Commodity flow modelling. Transportation research board. http://-onlinepubs.trb.org/onlinepubs/circulars/ec011/black.pdf

Brogan JD (1979) Development of truck trip-generation rates by generalized land use categories. *Transportation Research Record* 716: 38–43

Cherrett T, Allen J, McLeod F, Maynard S, Hickford A, Browne M (2012) Understanding urban freight activity – key issues for freight planning. *Journal of Transport Geography* 24: 22–32. CrossRef.

Comi A, Delle Site P, Filippi F, Nuzzolo A (2012) Urban freight transport demand modelling: A state of the art. *European Transport/Trasporti Europei* 51: 1–17

Ducret R, Gonzalez-Feliu J (2016) Connecting demand estimation and spatial category models for urban freight: First attempt and research implications. *Transportation Research Procedia* 12: 142–156. CrossRef.

Gasparini A (2008) Attractiveness of freight trip generators in urban areas. Master thesis. IME, Brazil. [in Portuguese]

Gonzalez-Feliu J, Routhier JL (2012) Modeling urban goods movement: How to be oriented with so many approaches? *Procedia - Social and Behavioral Sciences* 39: 89–100. CrossRef.

Holguín-Veras J, Jaller M, Sánchez-Díaz I, Wojtowicz J, Campbell S, Levinson H, Lawson C, Powers EL, Tavasszy L (2012) Freight trip generation and land use. National cooperative freight research program – NCFRP report 19. http://onlinepubs.trb.org/onlinepubs/nchrp/nchrp_rpt_739.pdf, accessed on 11 June 2015

Holguín-Veras J, Sánchez-Díaz I, Browne M (2016) Freight demand management: Role in sustainable urban freight system. *Transportation Research Procedia* 12: 40–52. CrossRef.

Holguín-Veras J, Sánchez-Díaz I, Lawson CT, Jaller M, Campbell S, Levinson HS, H-S S (2013) Transferability of freight trip generation models. *Transportation Research Record* 2397: 1–8. CrossRef.

IBGE – Instituto Brasileiro de Geografia e Estatística (2010) Population census 2010. Instituto brasileiro de geografia e estatística

Iding MHE, Meester WJ, Tavasszy LA (2002) Freight trip generation by firms. 42nd European congress of the European Regional Science Association, Dortmund, Germany

ITE – Institute of Transportation Engineers (2008) Trip generation handbook, an ITE recommended practice. Institute of transportation engineers, Washington, DC

Kulpa T (2014) Freight truck trip generation modelling at regional level. *Procedia - Social and Behavioral Sciences* 111: 197–202. CrossRef.

Marra C (1999) Chaaracterization of urban goods movements. Master thesis, UNICAMP, Brazil. [in Portuguese]

Melo IBC (2002) Demand assessment for freight transport in urban areas. Master thesis, IME, Rio de Janeiro

Ogden KW (1992) *Urban goods movement: A guide to policy and planning* (1st ed.). Ashgate Publishing, Burlington, VT

Oliveira LK (2014) Diagnosis of loading and unloading spaces for urban freight distribution: a case study in Belo Horizonte. *Journal of Transport Literature* 8: 178–209. CrossRef.

Oliveira LK, Guerra ED (2014) A diagnosis methodology for urban goods distribution: A case study in Belo Horizonte City (Brazil). *Procedia - Social and Behavioral Sciences* 125: 199–211. CrossRef.

Oliveira LK, Santos OR, Nóbrega RAA, Dablanc L (2016) The geography of warehousing in Belo Horizonte (Brazil). 14th World conference on transport research – WCTR 2016, Shanghai

Priya C, Ramadurai G, Devi G (2015) Freight trip generation models for Chennai, India. TRB 94th annual meeting compendium of papers, Washington, USA

Shin H, Kawamura K (2005) Data need for truck trip generation analysis: Qualitative analysis of the survey of retail stores. Transport Chicago, Illinois Institute of Technology

Silva MR, Waisman J (2007) Urban freight: an exploratory study about freight truck generation in bars and restaurants. 16th Brazilian congress of transport and traffic, Maceio, Brazil. [in Portuguese]

Sánchez-Díaz I, Holguín-Veras J, Wang X (2016) An exploratory analysis of spatial effects on freight trip attraction. *Transportation* 43: 177–196. CrossRef.

Souza CDR, Silva SD, D'Agosto MA (2010) Freight trip generators in urban areas. *Transportes* 18: 46–57. [in Portuguese]

Tadi RR, Balbach P (1994) Truck trip generation characteristics of nonresidential land uses. *ITE Journal* 64: 43–47